Frommer's

Dublin
day BY day™

2nd Edition

by Emma Levine

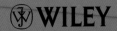

WILEY

A John Wiley and Sons, Ltd, Publication

Contents

UK Publisher: Sally Smith
Production Manager: Daniel Mersey
Commissioning Editor: Mark Henshall
Development Editor: Mary Anne Evans
Content Editor: Hannah Clement
Photo Research: Jill Emeny
Cartography: Tim Lohnes

Wiley also publishes its books in a variety of electronic formats. Some
content that appears in print may not be available in electronic books.

British Library Cataloguing in Publication Data

A catalogue record for this book is available from the British Library

ISBN: 978-0-470-74994-4 (pbk), ISBN: 978-0-470-975541 (ebk)

Typeset by Wiley Indianapolis Composition Services

Printed and bound in China by RR Donnelley

5 4 3 2 1

A Note from the Editorial Director

Organizing your time. That's what this guide is all about.

Other guides give you long lists of things to see and do and then expect you to fit the pieces together. The Day by Day guides are different. These guides tell you the best of everything, and then they show you how to see it *in the smartest, most time-efficient way*. Our authors have designed detailed itineraries organized by time, neighborhood, or special interest. And each tour comes with a bulleted map that takes you from stop to stop.

Hoping to tour the best in Georgian architecture, stroll down Grafton Street, or taste your way through gourmet Dublin? Planning a walk through Trinity College, or plotting a day of funfilled activities with the kids? Whatever your interest or schedule, the Day by Days give you the smartest routes to follow. Not only do we take you to the top attractions, hotels, and restaurants, but we also help you access those special moments that locals get to experience—those "finds" that turn tourists into travelers.

The Day by Days are also your top choice if you're looking for one complete guide for all your travel needs. The best hotels and restaurants for every budget, the greatest shopping values, the wildest nightlife—it's all here.

Why should you trust our judgment? Because our authors personally visit each place they write about. They're an independent lot who say what they think and would never include places they wouldn't recommend to their best friends. They're also open to suggestions from readers. If you'd like to contact them, please send your comments our way at feedback@frommers.com, and we'll pass them on.

Enjoy your Day by Day guide—the most helpful travel companion you can buy. And have the trip of a lifetime.

Warm regards,

Kelly Regan

Kelly Regan, Editorial Director
Frommer's Travel Guides

About the Author

Bradford-born and with Dublin roots, **Emma Levine** spent eight years living, working, and traveling in Asia as an author and photographer, specializing in cricket culture in India and Pakistan. Attention then turned to strange sports in Kyrgyzstan and Iran, and another book and TV series later she returned to England, and is now based in London. With itchy feet rarely soothed, Emma writes travel guides (and thankfully still travels) to far-flung cities around the world, still loving adventures and following sport. Emma is also the author and photographer of *Frommer's Istanbul Day by Day*.

Acknowledgments

Special thanks to Sinead Barden at Dublin Tourism, my tolerant host Ethel, and wonderful Dublin tour guide Heather (my cousin).

Star Ratings, Icons & Abbreviations

Every hotel, restaurant, and attraction listing in this guide has been ranked for quality, value, service, amenities, and special features using a star-rating system. Hotels, restaurants, attractions, shopping, and nightlife are rated on a scale of zero stars (recommended) to three stars (exceptional). In addition to the **star-rating system,** we also use a kids icon to point out the best bets for families. Within each tour, we recommend cafes, bars, or restaurants where you can take a break. Each of these stops appears in a shaded box marked with a coffee-cup-shaped bullet ☕.

The following **abbreviations** are used for credit cards:

AE	American Express	**DISC**	Discover	**V**	Visa
DC	Diners Club	**MC**	MasterCard		

Travel Resources at Frommers.com

Frommer's travel resources don't end with this guide. Frommer's website, **www.frommers.com,** has travel information on more than 4,000 destinations. We update features regularly, giving you access to the most current trip-planning information and the best airfare, lodging, and car-rental bargains. You can also listen to podcasts, connect with other Frommers.com members through our active-reader forums, share your travel photos, read blogs from guidebook editors and fellow travelers, and much more.

A Note on Prices

In the "Take a Break" and "Best Bets" sections of this book, we have used a system of dollar signs to show a range of costs for 1 night in a hotel (the price of a double-occupancy room) or the cost of an entree (main course) at a restaurant. Use the following table to decipher the dollar signs:

Cost	Hotels	Restaurants
$	under $100	under $10
$$	$100–$200	$10–$20
$$$	$200–$300	$20–$30
$$$$	$300–$400	$30–$40
$$$$$	over $400	over $40

How to Contact Us

In researching this book, we discovered many wonderful places—hotels, restaurants, shops, and more. We're sure you'll find others. Please tell us about them, so we can share the information with your fellow travelers in upcoming editions. If you were disappointed with a recommendation, we'd love to know that, too. Please write to:

Frommer's Dublin Day by Day, 2nd Edition
Wiley Publishing, Inc. • 111 River St. • Hoboken, NJ 07030-5774

13 Favorite
Moments

2

13 Favorite **Moments**

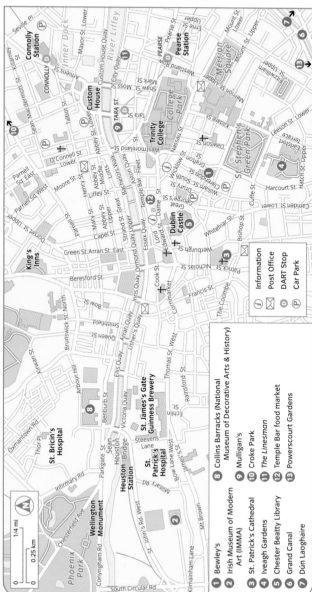

1 Bewley's
2 Irish Museum of Modern Art (IMMA)
3 St. Patrick's Cathedral
4 Iveagh Gardens
5 Chester Beatty Library
6 Grand Canal
7 Dún Laoghaire
8 Collins Barracks (National Museum of Decorative Arts & History)
9 Mulligan's
10 Croke Park
11 *The Linesman*
12 Temple Bar food market
13 Powerscourt Gardens

Information
Post Office
DART Stop
Car Park

Previous page: Statue of Molly Malone.

I have seen Dublin's huge transformation from 1970s gloomy economy to 1990s buoyant Celtic Tiger, and its 21st-century incarnation with cutting-edge design and sophisticated wine-bars. But some things don't change, like the Croke Park crowds, love of a drink, and the cheerful cynicism of the government. Hopefully, my favorite moments will still be possible in another few decades.

1 Sipping coffee on Bewley's balcony. The tiny balcony overlooking Grafton Street is ideal for sipping coffee and watching the world swarm beneath. It's now one of Dublin's many venues serving a decent cup of strong coffee, but Bewley's was the first and will always be an icon. *See p 60.*

2 Discovering the IMMA's art collection. The 17th-century Royal Hospital Kilmainham, once housing retired soldiers, is now home to the Irish Museum of Modern Art. Wander round its vast courtyard and compact exhibition rooms, in what is a fine use for an old hospital. *See p 68.*

3 Watching the sunlight inside St. Patrick's Cathedral. Late afternoon usually means Evensong's organ rehearsals in this historic cathedral. As the late afternoon sun starts to dip, watch the glowing colors on the walls as the light shines through the stained-glass windows. *See p 11.*

4 Sauntering through wooded walks at Iveagh Gardens. So close to busy St. Stephen's Green and yet a world away, this secluded Victorian garden has a cascade, armless statues, rosarium, and shady woods—made for solitary afternoons. *See p 88.*

5 Musing the manuscripts at Chester Beatty Library. One of my favorite exhibitions and venues. Instead of snaking lines for the *Book of Kells*, step into the tranquil Sacred Traditions display of illuminated

Bewley's busy exterior.

manuscripts from the Qur'an, ancient Persian texts, and miniature paintings from India. *See p 14.*

6 Strolling along the Grand Canal. This walk is alongside the main road and yet this canal-side path seems miles away from traffic. Enjoy a Sunday morning as the city awakens and, if it's sunny, ducks waddle out and bask in the warmth. I love the ancient locks, weeping willows, and the view of Peppercanister Church from Huband Bridge. *See p 51.*

7 Smelling the sea air at Dún Laoghaire. When I was a kid, we would drive along the coast to watch the ferries dock in Dún Laoghaire. These days the speedy

The Croker Crowds.

DART, the wonderful coastal suburban train, makes the journey even better. Step off the train and start smelling the sea. *See p 152.*

⑧ Exploring the aisles at 'What's In Store'. A highlight of **Collins Barracks.** Now housing the National Museum of Decorative Arts and History, thousands of exhibits cram into tall display cases at the What's In Store section, from samurai swords to silver. On each visit I notice different treasures. *See p 57.*

⑨ Deciding where serves the best pint of Guinness. Need I say more? Guinness might be available the world over, but it really does taste better over here. **Mulligan's?** Cobblestone? Ryan's? Hard to tell, but it's always a mouthwatering moment watching the pint being pulled slowly and then settling, ready to be sunk. *See p 118.*

⑩ Joining the Croker crowds. I've enjoyed countless sporting venues around the world, but **Croke Park** for hurling or Gaelic football is one of the greatest. The fun starts when both sets of supporters clad in their team's shirts walk together up O'Connell Street, bar-hopping along the way. And the riot of color and noise when the teams emerge onto the pitch is spine-tingling stuff. *See p 131.*

⑪ Greeting the Linesman on the Liffey. I love life-sized sculptures, of which Dublin has many. Here, *The Linesman* hauls ropes from the Liffey at Sir John Rogerson Quay, probably noticing how much his surroundings have changed over the decades. *See p 54.*

⑫ Enjoying the 'foodie' culture. It's good to see Dublin taking all things gastronomic seriously, and food markets springing up. Visit the one in Temple Bar to choose cheeses, sample ciders, and cast your discerning eye over the homemade cookies. *See p 85.*

⑬ Walking to Powerscourt Gardens. The mile-long walk from Enniskerry village to the entrance of grandiose Powerscourt House is breathtaking, especially in the fall when the beech trees are awash with deep orange. *See p 148.* ●

Cheeses at Temple Bar food market.

The Best **in One Day**

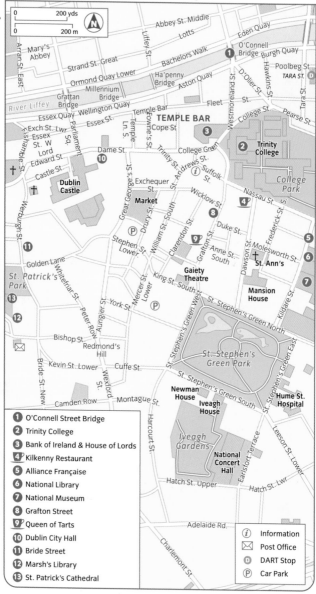

```
0        200 yds
0        200 m
```

1 O'Connell Street Bridge
2 Trinity College
3 Bank of Ireland & House of Lords
4 Kilkenny Restaurant
5 Alliance Française
6 National Library
7 National Museum
8 Grafton Street
9 Queen of Tarts
10 Dublin City Hall
11 Bride Street
12 Marsh's Library
13 St. Patrick's Cathedral

i Information
✉ Post Office
Ⓓ DART Stop
Ⓟ Car Park

Previous page: A wistful Oscar Wilde.

This full day kicks off with some of Dublin's most famous landmarks. You might not have the chance to see everything, but the beauty of compact Dublin is that you'll probably be retracing your steps on another day. It's a city for walking with scant need for public transport, so don your comfortable shoes—and waterproofs.
START: all cross-city buses to O'Connell St. LUAS: Abbey St.

1 ★ kids O'Connell Street Bridge. Stand on the north side of O'Connell Bridge by the statue of **Daniel O'Connell**, and you're in what many Dubliners believe is the very heart of the city. The man himself, cast impressively in bronze (see p 25, **11**), was a politician and patriot in the 1800s and the first Catholic to enter the House of Commons. Edge past the photo-snapping tourists and look for the bullet holes in the angels ringing the base of the statue. Look north to the immense, slender stainless steel **Millennium Spire** (commonly known as The Spike, see p 18, **5**) dominating the landscape, then cross the River Liffey over O'Connell Street Bridge. The bridge is unique in Europe: a multi-lane traffic highway, it is even wider than it is long. ⏱ **15 min. Bus: all cross-city buses.**

2 ★★ kids Trinity College. Ireland's oldest university, founded in 1592 by Queen Elizabeth I, is an oasis of lawns, cobbled paths, and myriad architectural styles ranging from the 1700s to the 1900s. Walk through the main entrance flanked by the two statues of old boys **Oliver Goldsmith** (1728–74) and **Edmund Burke** (1729–97), to the graceful white Campanile, a famous Dublin landmark. Explore the 16 hectares (40 acres) of grounds, and remember you're pacing the hallowed turf of an establishment that educated the likes of Oscar Wilde, Bram Stoker, and Samuel Beckett. There's probably a lengthy queue snaking around the huge Old Library to view the famous *Book of Kells*,

the illuminated manuscript dating back to A.D. 800. If you have time, I recommend returning another day to see Trinity and the *Book of Kells* in more detail. ⏱ **1 hr. See Special Interest Tours: Trinity College, p 36.**

3 ★★ Bank of Ireland & House of Lords. Opposite Trinity, the sweeping colonnade marks the entrance to the Bank of Ireland. It was originally constructed in 1729 as the House of Commons—the first purpose-built Parliament House in the world. Designed by Edward Pearce, later knighted, it was converted into the banking HQ following the 1800 Act of Union, which meant that the country would be governed from London. The House of Lords still survives; visit its oak-paneled interior to check out the huge 18th-century chandelier with more than 1,000 pieces of crystal,

Edmund Burke guards the college.

Dublin Pass

This smartcard gives you free entry to more than 30 top attractions, including Dublin Castle, Dublin Zoo, Guinness Storehouse, GAA Museum, The Shaw Birthplace, and St. Patrick's Cathedral. For those attractions that have free admission anyway, the Pass offers other benefits and discounts. Buy online (allow time for postage) or at Dublin Tourism's head office on Suffolk Street. If you buy at Dublin Airport's tourist office in the arrivals hall, it includes a free bus journey by Aircoach to the city center. The Dublin Pass (www.dublinpass.ie) is valid for 1 (€35), 2 (€55), 3 (€65), or 6 days (€95), with reductions for children.

and tapestries depicting historical scenes. The curator is usually on hand to give you good information. ⏱ 30 min. 2 College Green. ☎ 01-677 6801 ext 3369. Free admission. Mon–Wed & Fri 10am–4pm; Thurs 10am–5pm. 30-min guided tours Tues 10:30am, 11:30am & 12:30pm. Bus: all cross-city buses.

4 ★ kids **Kilkenny Restaurant.** Located in the Kilkenny store (see p 82) (you'll be tempted to return for a gift-buying spree), this is

The colonnaded Bank of Ireland.

perfect for good value coffee, cakes, home-made casseroles, or even a full Irish breakfast. It also has gluten-free dishes, which seem the norm now in Dublin. 5/6 Nassau St. ☎ 01-677 7075. $.

5 ★ **Alliance Française.** Pop around the corner to the Alliance Française (no. 1), previously the gentlemen's Kildare Street Club from the 1850s. Look closely at its exterior walls to see the O'Shea Brothers' (stonemasons extraordinaire who also worked on Trinity College) cheeky carvings of monkeys playing billiards: a social comment on the 'monkeys' in the club? ⏱ 10 min. 1 Kildare St.

6 ★★ **National Library.** Opened in 1890, this holds more than 1,000 manuscripts and nearly 100,000 books, including rare first editions of Joyce and Yeats. But there's more to it than books—go for the magnificent stained-glass windows in the entrance depicting luminaries in the worlds of literature and philosophy like Chaucer and Dante, the original marble staircase, and Harry Clarke's ornate stained-glass windows (see also Café Bar Deli at Bewley's, p 102) at the top of

the steps. Inside its vast domed reading room, today's scholars might use laptops but it's easy to visualize the same scene from a century ago. It's open to visitors Monday to Friday 9:30am to 12:30pm, although you won't be able to walk between the tables. If you're keen to trace your Irish roots, head to the **Genealogy Service** where expert staff can help you out. The library also has exhibition rooms and a decent cafe, plus occasional lunchtime literary events.
🕐 *30 min. Kildare St.* 📞 *01-603 0200. www.nli.ie. Free admission. Mon–Wed 9:30am–9pm; Thurs & Fri 9:30am–5pm; Sat 9:30am–1pm. Bus: inc 7, 8, 10, 11.*

7 ★★★ **kids** **National Museum.** One of Dublin's three National Museums (all of them free), this one is devoted to archaeology. At the main entrance, don't miss the intricate mosaic floor depicting the 12 signs of the zodiac. Once inside, highlights include Iron Age bog bodies discovered in 2003; amazingly preserved, you can still see the leather-plaited armband with a Celtic ornament on one of the bodies. The Treasury has exhibits from the early Middle Ages, considered the Golden Age of Irish Art, including the renowned Ardagh Chalice and Tara Brooch. Kids can pick up activity sheets from the ticket office. When you've finished exploring

Impressive door knocker to the National Museum.

the comfortably small museum, stand and look out from the wrought-iron balcony over the entire hall. 🕐 *1½ hr. See p 41,* **1**

8 ★★★ **kids** **Grafton Street.** It's time for a walk down Dublin's famous pedestrianized and fashionable street—usually packed. Once it was Irish stores dominating consumers' choice; these days it's well-known British chain stores like Accessorize and Marks & Spencer. Its southern end, at the entrance to St. Stephen's Green, is dominated by the grand **Royal Fusiliers' Arch**. Mid-way down, stop at **Bewley's** (see p 102), a famous coffee haven

Quiet please! The National Library reading room.

since 1840 and little changed since then. Grafton Street is also the unofficial venue for myriad buskers, from Romanian accordionists to Irish fiddlers and wannabe rock stars—the best ones usually playing early evening or at night. Throughout the day, especially during summer, you're likely to come across a scattering of human 'statues', costumed, spray-painted, and standing very still on a box—something that, quite remarkably, gets people giving money. Take a closer look at the (mainly) Georgian facades of the stores, most of which were originally built as private residences. At the northern end, you are greeted by the Tart with the Cart, Dolly with the Trolley, or Trollop with the Scallops. Get the idea? Poor **Molly Malone**'s (p 59, ❶) ample cleavage did everything to encourage unkind nicknames. ⏲ *30 min. All buses to St. Stephen's Green.*

9️⃣ ★★ kids Queen of Tarts. Indulge in freshly baked chocolate scones and quiche, hearty breakfast, or warming soups in this larger branch of the cute tea house, with large terrace. A real gem. *Cow's Lane, off Dame St.* ☎ *01-633 4681.$.*

❿ **★★ Dublin City Hall.** The huge Georgian rotunda of City Hall, recently restored, is breathtaking. Built in 1769 as headquarters for the city's merchants, it lies close to the trading hub of Dame Street (most likely the street you walked down), and is now used as council chambers. Its domed roof is embellished with gold leaf, and surrounded by four immense statues including one of Daniel O'Connell. The marble mosaic floor depicts Dublin's coat of arms with the daunting motto 'Happy the city where citizens obey'. Down in the restored vaults is the interesting **Story of the Capital** multimedia exhibition. Divided into three sections, it covers Dublin's history from Viking times, through Georgian, and up to the present day. ⏲ *1 hr. See p 44,* ❿.

⓫ **★ Bride Street.** If you're walking from City Hall to Marsh's Library, cut down Bride Street and pass Bull Alley on your right. This, like much of the area, was known for its redbrick Victorian housing for the city's poor (now Liberties College), financed by philanthropist Lord Iveagh (Cecil Guinness; 1847–1927). On the left, and around the corner onto Golden Lane, look up at the

Impressive statues circle City Hall's rotunda

Leather-bound journals in Marsh's Library.

apartments, where scenes from Jonathan Swift's novel *Gulliver's Travels* are carved in relief on the upper levels. ⏱ *15 min. Bus: 50, 54A, 56A.*

⑫ ★★ **Marsh's Library.** A bibliophile's dream. Founded in 1701 by the splendidly named Archbishop Narcissus Marsh, this was Ireland's first public library and amazingly is still in use. It's usually pretty empty, save for a couple of helpful staff, so you can marvel at the leather-bound tomes filling floor-to-ceiling dark oak bookcases. Look out for **Jonathan Swift**'s death mask and the desk at which he's thought to have written *Gulliver's Travels*. At the far end are the wired alcoves, or cages, where scholars were locked in with their rare books, preventing pilfering. This really is a living library; all the collection's 25,000 books, published between the 16th and 18th centuries, are now catalogued and available on the Internet. Visitors and researchers may request any book in advance and staff will have it ready for your visit; be prepared to wear protective gloves if the book is valuable. ⏱ *30 min. St. Patrick's Close.* ☎ *01-454 3511. www.marsh library.ie. Admission: €2.50 adults, €1.50 students & seniors, under 16s free. Mon & Wed–Fri 10am–1pm & 2–5pm; Sat 10am–1pm. Bus: 50, 54A, 56A.*

⑬ ★★ **kids** **St. Patrick's Cathedral.** Late afternoon is usually the best time to visit Ireland's largest church: the organ and choir often have a hearty practice before **Evensong** at 5:45pm, which even the irreligious would find spiritually uplifting, especially when shafts of sunlight glow through the stained-glass windows. St. Patrick (who was from Britain) baptized converts from paganism to Christianity close to here, and a small wooden church was built in his honor. The current cathedral dates from the 13th century and has been rebuilt many times since. Writer **Jonathan Swift** was its most famous dean, from 1713 to 1745. Look out for his grave and epitaph near the main entrance, standing up and facing the altar, relocated from a spot in the cathedral prone to flooding from the Poddle river. Still famous for its loud-pealing bells, the cathedral's choir took part in the first performance of **Handel's** *Messiah* in 1742. If the daily (Anglican) services don't appeal, try the organ recitals on most Wednesday evenings. Look out for volunteer guides for your own free guided tour. ⏱ *1 hr. St. Patrick's Close.* ☎ *01-475 4817. www.stpatrickscathedral.ie. Admission: €5 adults, €4 students, seniors, children 15 and under. Free admission to services. Mon–Fri 9am–5pm; Sat & Sun: (Mar–Oct) 9am–5:30pm, (Nov–Feb) Sat 9am–5pm; Sun 9am–3pm. No admission during Sun services; 10:45am–12:30pm & 2:45–4:30pm.* ☎ *01-453 9472 for other service times. Bus: 50, 54A, 56A.*

The Best **in Two Days**

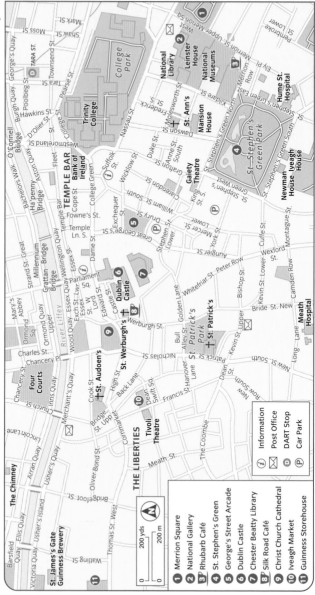

1 Merrion Square
2 National Gallery
3 Rhubarb Café
4 St. Stephen's Green
5 George's Street Arcade
6 Dublin Castle
7 Chester Beatty Library
8 Silk Road Café
9 Christ Church Cathedral
10 Iveagh Market
11 Guinness Storehouse

(i) Information
⊠ Post Office
Ⓓ DART Stop
Ⓟ Car Park

0   200 yds
0   200 m

After a full first day, the pace doesn't slow, although you can choose whether it's an in-depth visit or a quick look at many of these attractions. We explore a similar area to the previous tour, beginning with a taste of Georgian Dublin. It's another day bringing you the best of art, history, and churches—finishing up with a pint of Guinness with a rather special view. START: **Bus 4, 5, 7 & 45 to Merrion Square.**

1 ★★ kids Merrion Square. One of Dublin's most elegant Georgian squares, this was considered—and still is—the most noble part of the city. Wander through the neat lawns and trees of its interior, **Archbishop Ryan Park** (see p 32, **2**) and look out for the sculpture of **Oscar Wilde** reclining and gazing wistfully towards his childhood home, 1 Merrion Square (now the American University). Three sides of the square are lined with beautifully preserved Georgian houses, including Number Twenty Nine house museum (p 32, **3**). The square's railings are the venue for the weekend **Art Market** (p 83, busy in summer. *See also p 33,* **1**. ⏲ *45 min. Bus: 7, 10, 45.*

2 ★★ kids National Gallery. I often find that lines and crowds can spoil a gallery. Not so here. This one is spacious and relatively quiet—surprising considering some of the fantastic European art. Irish painting is well represented, especially its 17th-century re-emergence thanks to Jack B. Yeats. Highlights of the Italian School include masterpieces by Fra Angelico, Caravaggio, and Rubens. Huge works by Vermeer, Caravaggio, and Goya are my personal favorites, especially Caravaggio's *Taking of Christ*. Picasso, Monet, and Signac make up the French 20th-century school. Free activity packs are available for kids of all ages. ⏲ *1½ hr. Merrion Square West.* ☎ *01-661 5133. www.nationalgallery.ie. Free admission.*

Mon–Sat 9:30am–5:30pm; Thurs 9:30am–8:30pm; Sun noon–5:30pm. Bus: 5, 10, 44.

3 kids Rhubarb Café. This little eatery is one of Dublin's many friendly cafes with coffee, paninis, and cakes. Small and cozy with a couple of outdoor tables, it gets busy at lunchtimes with local office workers. Closed Sun. *18a Upper Merrion St.* ☎ *01-631 4924. $.*

4 ★★ kids St. Stephen's Green. This city center park was once the private gardens for local residents, each requiring a key to enter. Landscaped by the head of Guinness in 1880, it's since been a great public space with a huge pond where children feed the ducks, a bandstand with music performances in summer (look out for posters

The calm pond at St Stephen's Green.

outside), a small amphitheater, and sculptures and statues of prominent Dubliners. On sunny days, expect to see suited office-goers and students sprawled happily on the grass (which, strictly speaking, is not allowed). ⏰ 1 hr. See Chapter 5, p 88.

5 ★ kids George's Street Arcade. Dublin's first (and only) purpose-built Victorian shopping arcade, trade has fluctuated here since its opening in 1881. Formerly a meat market (the present-day Market Bar was once a sausage factory), these days it houses a quirky array of second-hand books, funky clothes, locally designed jewelry, deli-type foodstuff, cafes, and memorabilia. Gaze at its beautiful wrought-iron roof, gently restored to keep the original style, and the ornate red-brick Victorian facade on South Great George's Street. ⏰ 30 min. Entrances on Drury St. & South Great George's St. www.georges streetarcade.ie. Mon–Sat 9am–6:30pm; Thurs 9am–8pm; Sun noon–6pm (not all stalls open on Sun). Bus: 56A, 77, 123.

6 ★★ kids Dublin Castle. Located in one of Dublin's oldest areas, the castle's turbulent past encompasses Viking history, British

An opulent room in Dublin Castle.

rule, fires and rebellions, and most of it has been rebuilt. Enter via the main gateway to the Great Courtyard (remains from the original castle built by King John of England in 1204), and gaze up at the Record Tower, the last intact medieval tower in Dublin. Visits are by guided tour only to the opulent rooms, including the State Rooms with a throne used for royal visits, and the huge mahogany table used for diplomatic get-togethers. This table witnessed talks on the Good Friday (Belfast) Agreement, the 1998 groundbreaking treaty that finally brought peace to Northern Ireland. My personal favorite is St. Patrick's Hall, the ceremonial centerpiece with ceiling paintings and family crests, used for inaugurating Irish presidents. (See also *Vikings and Medieval Dubh Linn p 40*.) ⏰ 1 hr. Dame St. ☎ 01-645 8813. www. dublincastle.ie. Admission: €4.50 adults, €3.50 concs, €2 children aged 6–12, under 6s free. Tours: May–Sept every 20 min; Oct–April every 30–40 min. Bus: 49, 77, 123.

7 ★★★ Chester Beatty Library. The garden at the back of Dublin Castle leads to this wonderful gallery. Bequeathed by art collector Sir Arthur Chester Beatty, it exhibits treasures from world cultures and religions. I especially love the serene *Sacred Traditions Gallery* with illuminated centuries-old copies of the Qur'an, 12th-century Christian manuscripts, and intricately carved Japanese boxes. There's also a timeline of world religions since 3000 B.C. The *Arts of the Book* gallery tells of the achievements of Beatty himself, and his richly bound books including those for Marie-Antoinette. ⏰ 1½ hr. Dublin Castle. ☎ 01-407 0750. www.cbl. ie. Free admission. Mon–Fri 10am–5pm; Sat 11am–5pm; Sun 1–5pm; Oct–Apr closed Mon. Bus: 49, 77, 123.

8 **kids** **Silk Road Café.** Inside the library, this spacious cafe enjoys Middle Eastern chefs' creations, all at great value. Choose from dishes like moussaka, or Turkish chicken, and fresh salads, or just coffee and sweet baklava. *Dublin Castle.* ☎ *01-407 0770. www.silkroadcafe.ie. $.*

9 ★ **kids** **Christ Church Cathedral.** One of Dublin's oldest landmarks, the cathedral dates back to 1030 although the present structure was built in the 1870s. Its aisles have seen many a congregant here, from Norman warrior, Strongbow—who rebuilt it in stone and you can see a monument to him—to William of Orange, who donated treasures after his Battle of the Boyne victory in 1690. The cathedral choir took part in the world's first performance of **Handel's** *Messiah* in 1742, along with the choir from neighboring St. Patrick's. Its bells are the world's largest full-circle peal—listen out for their practice on Fridays 7pm to 9pm. ⏱ *1 hr. Christchurch Place.* ☎ *01-677 8099. www. cccdub.ie. Admission: €6 adults, €4 concs, under 16s free. Jun–Aug 9am–6pm; Sept–May 9:45am–5 or 6pm. Sun 12:30–2:30pm & 4:30–6:15pm. Bus: 49, 50, 51B, 77.*

10 ★ **Iveagh Market.** Walk down Nicholas St. to the old Iveagh Market, built by Lord Iveagh in 1906 and now in disrepair. There were rumors of renovation, but we won't hold our breath for that. Look up to see the impish portrait on the corner, giving a cheeky wink, thought to be none other than the founder himself. *Between Francis St., Dean Swift Sq & Lamb Alley.*

11 ★ **kids** **Guinness Storehouse.** Firmly on the tourist trail, this former fermentation plant is in the heart of St. James's Gate

The Guinness Store House has been churning out the 'black stuff' since 1759.

Brewery which has churned out Guinness since 1759. If you walk up Crane Street, dating back to 1728, look down cobbled Rainsford Street (1700) to spot the original tram lines. Inside, it's huge, crowded, and lots of fun, and where the story of the history, production, and advertizing of the black stuff is told. Look out for the Tasting Laboratory explaining how different parts of the tongue taste its various elements. The second floor houses the famous advertising campaigns from the 1980s, although I prefer John Gilroy's 1930–60 ads. Your ticket includes a free pint of Guinness at the top-floor Gravity Bar, with 360° city views. Book online for a 10% discount, or pay at the credit card machines at the entrance to skip the lines. ⏱ *2 hr (including drink). St. James's Gate.* ☎ *01-408 4800. www.guinness-storehouse.com. Admission: €15 adults, €11 students over 18 & seniors, €9 students under 18, €5 children aged 6–12, free for children under 6; €34 family ticket. May–Sept 9:30am–7pm (last admission); Oct–Apr 9:30am–5pm (last admission). Bus: 51B, 78A, 123.*

The Best **in Three Days**

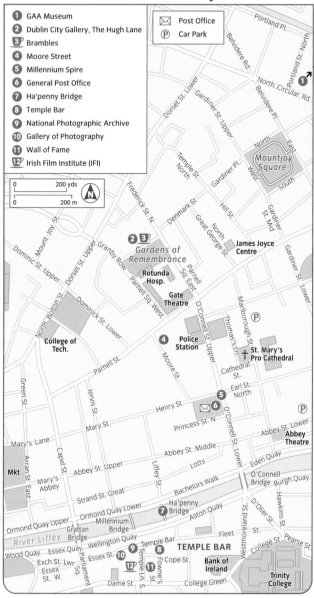

1 GAA Museum
2 Dublin City Gallery, The Hugh Lane
3 Brambles
4 Moore Street
5 Millennium Spire
6 General Post Office
7 Ha'penny Bridge
8 Temple Bar
9 National Photographic Archive
10 Gallery of Photography
11 Wall of Fame
12 Irish Film Institute (IFI)

⊠ Post Office
Ⓟ Car Park

I t's time to explore north of the River Liffey, starting in the wonderful Croke Park for a unique sporting experience. Enjoy the hearty walk to famous O'Connell St, ending the day at Temple Bar. You'll also be passing through busy shopping areas, so it's your choice how much time—and money!—you wish to spend. START: **Bus: 3, 11, 16 or 46A from O'Connell Street to Croke Park.**

❶ ★★★ kids GAA Museum. As a huge sports fan, this is a personal favorite. Inside the Croke Park Stadium and HQ of the Gaelic Athletic Association, which celebrated its 125th anniversary in 2009, the museum tells the story of Gaelic games, especially hurling and Gaelic football. A 15-minute video at the start of the tour demonstrates the furious pace of hurling, at which point you realize what soft sports soccer and basketball really are. It's also clear to see why Gaelic games have had a strong presence in Irish heroic literature since the 18th century. The museum exhibits players' jerseys, photos, and trophies dating back to 1871, and activities like hitting the ball with the hurley (like a hockey stick). Take the guided stadium tour to walk through the dressing rooms, VIP section, and corporate levels, with its colorful history. My favorite moment is when the tour ends with a walk through the players' tunnel and onto the pitch. ⏱ *2 hr. Croke Park, access via St. Joseph's Ave.* ☎ *01-819 2323. www.crokepark.ie/ gaa-museum. Admission: €6 adults, €4.30 students & seniors, €4 children 11 and under; €16 family ticket. Museum & stadium tour: €11 adults, €8.50 students & seniors, €7.50 children 11 and under; €30 family ticket. Mon–Sat 9:30am–5pm, Sun & p/hols noon–5pm. Jul & Aug: Mon–Sat 9:30am–6pm. Tours: every hour Mon–Sat 10am–3pm, Sun 1pm–3pm. Nov–Feb Mon–Fri 11am, 1pm & 3pm. Jul & Aug last tour 4pm. Bus: 3, 11, 16 from O'Connell St.*

Stadium tour of Croke Park.

❷ ★★ Dublin City Gallery, The Hugh Lane. It's around a half-hour walk southwest from Croke Park, so this spacious gallery is a good place to relax. Better known as Hugh Lane Gallery, this has many Irish artists on display in a collection exceeding 2,000 pieces. Impressionist masterpieces include Manet's *Le Concert aux Tuileries,* Monet's *Waterloo Bridge,* and Renoir's *Les Parapluies* but check out Irish painters, especially Sean Scully's abstract creations and Jack B. Yeats's oils. The highlight is the **Francis Bacon Collection,** including the recreation of his London studio with paint-encrusted walls, and scattered with piles of cans, dirty paintbrushes, and canvases. (If you thought you had an untidy house, look at his studio. It's great to know that such genius can indeed emerge from chaos) The gallery also hosts Sunday lectures and free concerts (see p 127). ⏱ *1 hr. Charlemont House, Parnell Square North.* ☎ *01-222 5550. www.hughlane.ie. Free admission. Tues–Thurs 10am–6pm, Fri & Sat 10am–5pm, Sun 11am–5pm. Bus: 3, 10, 13.*

3 **kids** **Brambles.** In the gallery's basement, this bijoux cafe looks out onto the tiny garden courtyard. Relax with a gourmet wrap or roulade and a glass of wine. *Hugh Lane Gallery, Parnell Square North.* ☎ *01-222 5550. $.*

4 ★ **Moore Street.** The once-famous street market has diminished in size and quality over time, but is still worth a look for an earthy Dublin shopping experience. (My late grandmother loved a bargain and came here for fruit and veg.) Some women still sell bric-a-brac and the odd box of apples from old-fashioned prams. Its vendors now reflect Dublin's changing population, with more Asian and African stallholders selling foodstuff from sunnier climes. Look out for horse-and-carts doing their morning delivery, and listen out for local bawdy banter. ⏱ *30 min. Moore St. Mon–Sat 8am–4pm. Bus: all buses to O'Connell St.*

5 ★★ **Millennium Spire.** Replacing Nelson's Column, blown up in 1966 by the IRA, the Spire was the result of a long drawn-out planning process—three years late in welcoming the Millennium. Although most Dubliners think it's a total waste of money (€5 million), the 120m (395 ft) high stainless steel spire, 3m (10 ft) wide at the base and tapering to 15cm (6 inches) at the top, is the tallest city center structure and impossible to

The Millennium Spire has several nicknames including 'Stiletto in the Ghetto' and 'Poker near Croker'.

miss. Its color changes: metallic blue at sunrise and sunset; shiny gray in the day; and black at night with tiny lights on the upper sections. Dubliners love their nicknames: the more repeatable ones for this include the Spire in the Mire, Stiletto in the Ghetto, and Poker near Croker. ⏱ *10 min. Bus: all buses to O'Connell St.*

6 ★★ **General Post Office.** The GPO sits prominently on O'Connell Street, not only a national institution but also central to the political and military turmoil of the 1916 Rising. Designed by Francis Johnston and built in 1814, its distinctive Doric columns span the five central bays, with John Smyth's statues of Fidelity, Hibernia, and Mercury above the portico. While buying your stamps inside the huge hall, take a look at the beautifully elaborate ceiling with Grecian designs. *See also p 25,* **10**. ⏱ *10 min. An Post, O'Connell St.*

Free admission. Counters open Mon–Sat 8am–8pm.

7 ★ kids **Ha'penny Bridge.** The first pedestrian bridge over the River Liffey (and the only one until 2000) this iron bridge was built in 1816 and is a much-loved symbol of Dublin. Officially called the Liffey Bridge, and before that Wellington Bridge, its nickname came from the half-penny tax charged for each pedestrian to cross, which continued until 1919. Local folklore suggests that the tax was to keep the northern 'riff-raff' away from the cultured Southside. (There still remains some rivalry between those born in the north and south, the latter seeing themselves as superior.) The loveliest time is in the late afternoon sun with pedestrians' long shadows cast onto the side rails, or illuminated at night. ⏱ *10 min. Bus: all buses to O'Connell St. LUAS: Abbey St.*

8 ★★ kids **Temple Bar.** The south side of the bridge brings you to Temple Bar, a regenerated area and home to arts and entertainment since the early 1990s. Previously a forgotten edge of dockland, cheap rents brought an influx of the bohemian type, and so now there are

Sculptural detail on the General Post Office building.

bars, theaters, live music venues, and galleries aplenty. It's also the location of several weekend markets (see Chapter 4, Shopping). Most streets are narrow, cobbled and with little traffic, so it's a delightful area to explore. Fridays to Sundays it's usually packed with raucous Hen and Stag parties (mainly from England), changing the ambience to a drinking fest (fancy-dress optional), with buskers and

Illuminated Ha'Penny Bridge.

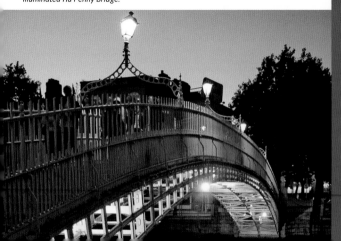

Explore the bars, theatres and music venues in Temple Bar.

street performers. ⏱ *30 min. www. templebar.ie.*

⑨ ★★ National Photographic Archive. Part of the National Library's collection, this small gallery is home to more than 630,000 photographs, predominantly Irish, with regularly changing exhibitions from its collection. Most of the negatives and transparencies have come from postcard and portrait studios throughout 20th-century Ireland and cast a fascinating light on the nation's past. Visitors may access the archive, and its little store has books and postcards. ⏱ *40 min. Meeting House Square, Temple Bar.* ☎ *01-603 0374. www.nli. ie. Free admission. Mon–Fri 10am– 5pm, Sat 10am–2pm. Bus: all buses to Dame St. or Wellington Quay.*

⑩ ★★ Gallery of Photography. Ireland's main photography venue, its regularly changing exhibitions showcase prominent Irish and international contemporary photographers. It's also a chance for a surprise look at classic 20th-century photojournalists (I saw Josef Koudelka on my last visit). Made up of small white-walled exhibition rooms, it's a striking and bijou exhibition space. ⏱ *30 min. Meeting*

House Square, Temple Bar. ☎ *01- 671 4654. www.galleryofphotography. ie. Free admission. Tues–Sat 11am– 6pm; Sun 1–6pm. Bus: all buses to Dame St. or Wellington Quay.*

⑪ ★ kids Wall of Fame. This external wall covered with huge photos captures the great and the good in Irish music. Taken mainly during the 1970s and 1980s by Irish photographers, artists range from the Pogues' Shane McGowan (suitably clutching a bottle of booze), Van Morrison, the late Phil Lynott, an unangelic-looking Bob Geldof, and of course U2, Ireland's most successful export. Stand on the street in the evening when the photos are lit up for the best view, better still if there is a guitarist busking nearby. ⏱ *10 min. Temple Lane South. www.wall offame.ie. Bus: all buses to Dame St. or Wellington Quay.*

⑫ Irish Film Institute (IFI). A film buff's haven, the spacious and relaxing cafe bar serves tasty burgers, pasta, and pies at lunch-times and evenings. Fantastic value. *IFI, 6 Eustace St., Temple Bar.* ☎ *01-679 5744.$.* ●

Dublin's **Heroes**

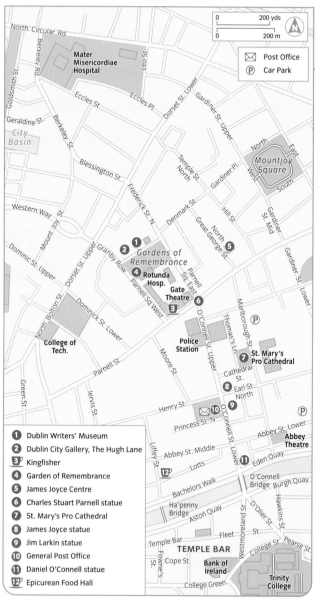

1. Dublin Writers' Museum
2. Dublin City Gallery, The Hugh Lane
3. Kingfisher
4. Garden of Remembrance
5. James Joyce Centre
6. Charles Stuart Parnell statue
7. St. Mary's Pro Cathedral
8. James Joyce statue
9. Jim Larkin statue
10. General Post Office
11. Daniel O'Connell statue
12. Epicurean Food Hall

Previous page: Georgian architecture in Dublin.

Dublin is renowned for its heroes, an endless list comprising political and creative luminaries who shaped the city, and this tour around O'Connell Street offers a flavor of both. But you'll find countless more examples during your stay, especially those heroes celebrated in the form of attractive statues and sculptures which dot the city. START: **Bus 11, 13 & 16 to Eccles St.**

① ★ **Dublin Writers' Museum.** This is your best chance for an insight into the lives of great Dublin writers all under one gorgeous Georgian roof, revealing 300 years of great Irish literature. Quirky memorabilia include a colorful postcard from Los Angeles written by Brendan Behan, Samuel Beckett's telephone, letters from Yeats, and early editions of *Waiting for Godot* and *Dracula*. There are also priceless nuggets of info such as Oscar Wilde's boxing prowess. Expressive marble sculptures and portraits on the top floor include a noble Jonathan Swift, plus a more contemporary Christy Brown. ⏱ *1 hr. 18 Parnell Square.* ☎ *01-872 2077. www.writersmuseum.com. Admission: €7.50 adults, €6.30 concs, €4.70 children 11 and under. Mon–Sat 10am–5pm; Sun & p/hols 11am–5pm.*

② ★★ **Dublin City Gallery, The Hugh Lane.** Sir Hugh Lane, the founder of this gallery containing art from Ireland and further afield, was a fascinating hero. He finally fulfilled his deep desire to open a Dublin modern art gallery, persuading leading artists to donate pieces. It opened in 1908 in Harcourt Street, but a few years later Lane himself was killed on board the *RMS Lusitania*, which sank after being hit by a German torpedo. A dispute followed with London's National Gallery over the rightful home of the paintings, because Lane had changed his will without it being witnessed. Happily a compromise was eventually reached. Don't miss the chaotically messy recreated studio of Dublin-born Francis Bacon. ⏱ *1 hr. See p 17,* **②***.*

Dublin Writers' Museum.

③ ★ **Kingfisher.** Depending on what time you get here, choose from fresh fish and chips or full Irish breakfast served with charming hospitality, popular with locals and builders. *166 Parnell St.* ☎ *01-872 8732. $.*

④ ★ **Garden of Remembrance.** Before hitting busy O'Connell Street, take time out to relax in this tranquil garden, opened in 1966 to commemorate the 50th anniversary of the Easter Rising and all those who died during the struggle for Irish freedom. It's dominated by the cross-shaped water feature, leading the eye to Oisin Kelly's immense cast-iron sculpture which is based on the theme of the *Children of Lir*, its birds in flight symbolizing rebirth and resurrection. ⏱ *15 min. East Parnell Square.*

❺ ★★ James Joyce Centre.

Here's a chance to learn about Joyce's life—and get your head around his 'stream of consciousness' method of writing especially at the interactive *James Joyce & Ulysses* exhibition. The top floor is especially illuminating, recreating his studies in Trieste, Zurich, and Paris where he wrote *Ulysses* from 1914 to 1922. In fact, Joyce spent most of his life in exile. Difficult to believe that this much-lauded writer was at the time rejected by the Irish, who said he was 'politically incorrect' in his criticism of the middle-class Catholic establishment. At the back of the house, check out the original front door from 7 Eccles St. (which was around one mile north), the fictional home of Leopold Bloom from *Ulysses*. 🕐 1 hr. 35 North Great George's St. ☎ 01-878 8547. www.jamesjoyce.ie. Admission: €5 adults; €4 concs; free children 11 and under. Tues–Sat 10am–5pm, Sun noon–5pm.

❻ ★ Charles Stuart Parnell statue.

The bronze statue of Parnell, born to a wealthy Protestant land-owner in 1846, dominates the northern end of O'Connell Street. After being elected to parliament in 1878, he opposed the Irish land laws and became the accepted leader of the Irish nationalist movement. Advocating a boycott to influence landlords, he was sent to Kilmainham. After his release he joined the Liberal party, which successfully introduced the first Irish Home Rule Bill. Sadly Parnell's reputation was ruined when his long-standing affair with Kitty O'Shea (with whom he had three children) surfaced when her husband filed for divorce. 🕐 10 min. Corner of Upper O'Connell St. & Parnell St.

❼ ★ St. Mary's Pro Cathedral.

The modest colonnaded entrance of Dublin's main Catholic church is tucked away from the city's hub—yet it should have been built where the current GPO stands. Inside, look out for the 2006 statue by Timothy Schmalz dedicated to The Venerable Matt Talbot (1856–1925), considered the 'Holy Man of Dublin'. With his young life devoted to the demon drink, he pledged to God aged 28 that he would never again touch alcohol. True to his word, he abstained and also attended daily mass at this cathedral. After his death in 1925, he was considered a saintly man and a protector of all those suffering from addiction. 🕐 15 min. 83 Marlborough St. ☎ 01-874 5441. www.procathedral.ie. Free admission. Mon–Sat 7:30am–7pm, Sun 9am–1:45pm & 5:30–7:45pm.

❽ ★ James Joyce statue.

You've probably now seen the book (real or electronic), viewed his study, and seen his hero's door—now you can see what JJ looked like. This life-size sculpture portrays his characteristic nonchalant stance as he leans on his cane, thereby provoking the locals' unflattering nickname the Prick with the Stick. *Corner O'Connell St. & North Earl St.*

❾ ★ Jim Larkin statue.

Created by Oisin Kelly (see ❹, Garden of Remembrance), you can almost hear

Children of Lir in the Garden of Remembrance.

'Big Jim' rallying the troops, bronze arms outstretched as he stands between the GPO and Clery's. Liverpool-born Larkin (1874–1947) founded the Irish Transport & General Workers' Union. This strong union threatened the bosses and members were forced to leave, leading to the great lock-out of 1913 when 100,000 workers were sacked. The struggle continued for eight months. The feisty Scouser was the first leader of the Irish Labour party and continued campaigning for some of Ireland's poorest workers. *O'Connell St, between Clery's & GPO.*

⑩ ★★ General Post Office.

Probably one of the most politically significant post offices in the world, this was the focal point of the 1916 Easter Rising. The Irish Volunteers and Irish Citizen Army seized the building on Easter Monday—a day when many British troops were at the horse-racing in Fairyhouse, on the edge of the city. On these very steps, just before midday, the Proclamation of Independence was read by Pádraic Pearse. The rebels then remained inside for a week, until forced out by shelling from the British. One of the few remaining copies of the Declaration is on display inside the Philatelic Shop, to the right of the entrance. Visit the fascinating new exhibition here (scheduled to open mid-2010), featuring the history of the building. Oliver Sheppard's sculpture of legendary Irish warrior Cuchulainn, who inspired great terror in his enemies, sits in the main window looking out onto the street. Poke your finger in the pillars' bullet holes outside—apparently it brings good luck. *See p 18, ⑥.*

⑪ ★★ Daniel O'Connell statue.

Born into a Catholic family in 1775, O'Connell became a self-taught lawyer and politician and used his immense knowledge,

Daniel O'Connell Statue.

influence, and political beliefs to change the life of Irish Catholics for good. Not surprising that many called him 'the Liberator'. Previously they were forbidden to vote, study, join professions, or stand for parliament. Advocating non-violent political reform, he was committed to their emancipation and formed the Catholic Association in 1823. A year after winning election to the British Parliament—yet ironically unable to take a seat because of his religion—the Catholic Emancipation Act was passed, making O'Connell the uncrowned king of Ireland in many people's eyes (his crypt is a highlight in Glasnevin Cemetery, see p 48, ⑤). Befitting his status, the statue stands at one of the city's most visible points. *O'Connell St.*

⑫ ★ kids Epicurean Food Hall.

Finish off the day at one of the small stalls that circle this busy hall, cooking up multi-ethnic cuisine. Choose from Mexican tacos, pizza, Turkish meze, curries, or just toasted bagels with jam and coffee. Perfect for a snack or meal. *Entrances: Abbey St. & Liffey St.* ☎ *01-872 8732. $.*

Dublin with Kids

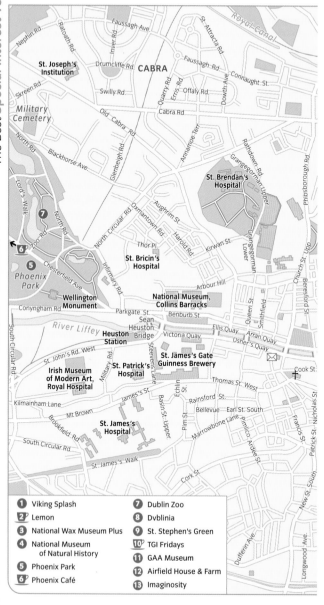

1	Viking Splash	**7**	Dublin Zoo
2	Lemon	**8**	Dvblinia
3	National Wax Museum Plus	**9**	St. Stephen's Green
4	National Museum of Natural History	**10**	TGI Fridays
5	Phoenix Park	**11**	GAA Museum
6	Phoenix Café	**12**	Airfield House & Farm
		13	Imaginosity

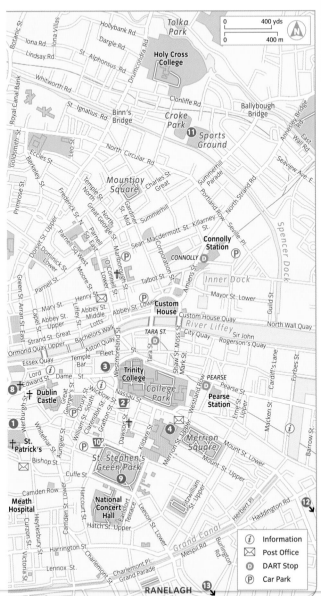

0	400 yds
0	400 m

Tolka Park

Holy Cross College

Hollybank Rd.
Dargle Rd.
St. Alphonsus Rd.
Iona Rd.
Iona Villas
Lindsay Rd.
Botanic Rd.
Whitworth Rd.
St. Ignatius Rd.
Binn's Bridge
Clonliffe Rd.
Ballybough Bridge
Anglesey Bridge
East Wall Rd.
Royal Canal Bank
Croke Park
⑪ Sports Ground
Seaview Ave. E.
North Circular Rd.
Goldsmith St.
Berkeley St.
Eccles St.
Leo St.
Mountjoy Square
Charles St. Great
Summerhill Parade
Portland Row
North Strand Rd.
Spencer Dock
Primrose St.
Temple St.
North Frederick St. N.
Great George
Gardiner St. Mid.
Summerhill
Sean Macdermott St.
Killarney St.
Seville Pl.
Dorset St. Upper
Dominick St. Lower
Parnell Sq. West
Parnell Sq. East
Moore St.
O'Connell St.
Marlborough St.
Connolly Station ℗
Inner Dock
Parnell St.
Mary St.
Henry St.
Abbey St. Upper
Abbey St. Middle
Talbot St.
Amiens St.
CONNOLLY Ⓓ
Mayor St. Lower
Guild St.
Capel St.
Arran St. East
Liffey St.
Lotts
Abbey St. Lower
Custom House
Custom House Quay
North Wall Quay
Strand St. Great
Bachelors Walk
River Liffey
Sir John Rogerson's Quay
Ormond Quay Upper
Aston Quay
City Quay
Cardiff's Lane
Essex Quay
Temple Bar
③
Fleet St.
Westmoreland St.
TARA ST. Ⓓ
Tara St.
Shaw St.
Moss St.
Mark St.
Forbes St.
Lord Edward St.
ⓘ
Dame St.
Trinity College
College Park
PEARSE Ⓓ
Pearse St.
⑧
Dublin Castle
George's St.
Wicklow St.
Nassau St.
Westland Row
Pearse Station
Macken St.
①
Werburgh St.
Whitefriar St.
Aungier St.
William St. South
Drury St.
Clarendon St.
Grafton St.
Dawson St.
Kildare St.
④
Merrion Square
Mount St. Lower
Erne St. Upper
ⓘ
St. Patrick's
Bishop St.
⑩ ℗
St. Stephen's Green Park
⑨
Merrion Row
Mount St. Upper
Barrow St.
Meath Hospital
Cuffe St.
Camden Row
National Concert Hall
Earlsfort Terrace
Hatch St. Upper
Leeson St. Lower
Fitzwilliam St. Upper
⑫
Camden St. Lower
Harcourt St.
Heytesbury St.
Curzon St.
Victoria St.
Harrington St.
Charlemont Pl.
Grand Parade
Grand Canal
Mespil Rd.
Burlington Rd.
Haddington Rd.
Herbert Pl.
Lennox St.
Charlemont St.
RANELAGH
⑬

ⓘ	Information
✉	Post Office
Ⓓ	DART Stop
℗	Car Park

From themed museums to vast parks, there's entertainment galore to keep the kids amused. Don't attempt to do all these in a day, just select venues suitable for their age and interest. To relax, Dublin's outdoor spaces are brilliant, and remember that the national museums and galleries all have activity packs for little ones. See also Chapter 5, The Best of the Outdoors. START: **All cross city buses to St. Stephen's Green.**

❶ ★ Viking Splash. This entertaining tour by land and sea led by a costumed guide gives an amusing take on the city, touching on its Viking history and also pointing out historic highlights. Traveling on a 'Duck'—a 7-tonne amphibious World War II tank—kids (and adults if they wish) get to wear Viking helmets and roar at passers-by. Endure the inevitable squeals as the tank then launches into the water for a tour around the Docklands. This tour is on the pricey side for adults. ⏱ 1 hr 15 min. *Pick-up points cnr Merrion Row & Dawson St., and cnr Patrick St. & Bull Alley. Office: 18 Mill St. Reservations recommended:* ☎ *01-707 6000. www.vikingsplash. ie. Admission €20 adults, €10*

Baby gorilla at Dublin Zoo.

children 12 and under. Daily every 2 hr 10am–5pm. Bus: all buses to St. Stephen's Green, or 49, 50, 51B, 77 for Patrick St.

❷ Lemon. Pancakes and waffles galore, both savory and sweet, from this cheerful orange-colored cafe. The ice-cream banana supreme crepe makes a yummy late-morning snack. *66 South William St.* ☎ *01-672 9044. $.*

❸ ★★ National Wax Museum Plus. This new four-floor museum, opened in late 2009, was previously home to Ireland's gold and arms store, but is now a thoroughly entertaining family attraction. Start in the Writers' Room where Brendan Behan sits, fittingly, drinking with Patrick Kavanagh, and you can press the green button on the wall to hear a narration and quotes related to their works and lives. Come face-to-face with life-sized models of early Irish leaders, or venture to the Chamber of Horrors with animatronic Dracula or creepy Hannibal Lector. The most popular kids' section is the interactive Irish Heroes of Discovery, paying homage to Irish inventors and scientists, chock-full of electronic experiments and touch-screen gadgets. Good early evening entertainment ⏱ 1½ hr. *The Armoury, Foster Place.* ☎ *01-671 8373. www.wax museumplus.ie. Thurs–Sat 10am–9pm. Admission €10 adults, €7 children 2–11 years, €30 family. Sun–Wed 10am–7pm. Bus: all buses to Dame St. inc 7b, 11b, 14, 16.*

④ ★★★ National Museum of Natural History. It's welcome back for this family favorite, known among locals as the 'Dead Zoo', reopened in April 2010 after extensive repairs following a stairwell collapse. That aside, it's held up well since its foundation in 1857, a veritable collectors' dream; as you enter, its wooden floorboards are loaded with giant deer, foxes, and insects, with large mammals—giraffe, elephant, and polar bear—calling the next floor up their home. Let the kids run riot along the narrow balconies, and explore the new education space. 🕐 *1 hr. Merrion St. Upper.* ☎ *01-677 7444. www.museum.ie. Free admission. Tues–Sat 10am–5pm; Sun 2–5pm. Bus: 44, 48.*

⑤ ★★★ Phoenix Park. The largest enclosed park in a European capital, this covers a mammoth 700 hectares (1,730 acres). It's impossible to walk the whole park with kids, but highlights include the **Visitors' Centre** near Ashtown Gate with a lovely exhibition of the park's history through the ages, with displays on the Viking grave discovered here and an interactive wildlife section for younger kids. **Bicycle Hire** inside the Parkgate Street main entrance includes child-sized bikes, tandems, and baby-carriers, giving the best chance to explore the park in all its green glory. Bring a picnic and make the most of the space. *See Chapter 5, The Best of the Outdoors.*

⑥ Phoenix Café. A huge outdoor courtyard caters for all ages, with drinks, cakes, meals, and snacks. It's a great space to relax, and also has tasty takeouts. *Visitors' Centre, Phoenix Park, Ashtown Gate.* ☎ *01-677 0090. $.*

⑦ ★ Dublin Zoo. Located inside Phoenix Park, the zoo has come a

Viking gods at Dublinia.

long way since its 1830s beginnings, and now its research and conservation is vital for endangered species. The African Plains section was created thanks to a 13-hectare (32-acre) extension given by the Government. Try to spot a tiger, white rhino, or zebra, and see the orangutan family at the World of Primates, whose history reads like something from a soap opera. My personal favorites, the Big Cats, are hard to spot thanks to the space they are able to inhabit, which I guess is the flip side of decent living conditions. There are several daily **Meet the Keeper** sessions during summer; October to February weekends only. Pick a dry day to enjoy its leafy surroundings. 🕐 *2 hr. Phoenix Park,* ☎ *01-474 8900. www.dublinzoo.ie. Admission: €15 adults; €12 concs; €10.50 children 4–15 years; from €43.50 family. Daily from 9:30am; closing time varies monthly; please check in advance. LUAS: Museum (red line); Bus: inc: 10, 25, 26, 66.*

⑧ ★★ Dvblinia. Step back into the Viking era in the heart of medieval Dublin, tracing the city's roots from its capture by Strongbow. Kids will love the recreated fairground with sound effects, medicine stalls (open the drawers to see the cures), and the invitation to throw balls at the man in the stocks. There are also lurid descriptions in the Death and Diseases display—including toilet paper made of moss. The History Hunters exhibition gets to grips with archaeology, exhibiting remains discovered near South Great George's Street including four Viking warrior skeletons with weapons. Ogle at the 900-year-old creepy skeleton and a wolf skull—amazing to think that Dublin was forest-covered in the 15th century. End with a 96-step climb up the 17th-century viewing tower in the adjacent St. Michael's Church, for a rare Dublin panoramic view. See also p 42, ④. ⏱ *1 hr.* *St. Michael's Hill, Christchurch.* ☎ *01-679 4611. www.dublinia.ie. Admission: €7 adults, €5.25 concs, €4.95 children 6–17 years, €20 family. Daily 10am–5pm (last entry 4pm). Bus: 50, 78A.*

⑨ ★ **St. Stephen's Green.** This bucolic expanse is a must for young kids to run around—and all adults enjoy feeding the ducks: walk to the pond, to the left of the Fusiliers' Arch entrance, and dispense with your leftover sandwiches. There's also a children's playground near the center of the green. It's easy to visualize when this was once prime pram-pushing territory back in Georgian times, such are the lovely willows, flowerbeds, and the general benefits of a green oasis in the city. During summer, there are occasional free plays performed in the amphitheater, and lunchtime music recitals in the bandstand. ⏱ *1 hr. See section St. Stephen's Green & Iveagh Gardens in Chapter 5 for details.*

🔟 **TGI Fridays.** When only a burger, pizza, or ice cream will do, this branch will satisfy a monster appetite. Coloring books and crayons keep little visitors entertained. *St. Stephen's Green West (also accessed via Stephen's Green Shopping Centre).* ☎ *01-478 1233. $$.*

⑪ ★★ **GAA Museum.** Any sporty kid will love the challenge of trying to hit the ball with the hurley (like a hockey stick) or kick the Gaelic football over the posts. Many of the

St. Stephen's Green.

One of many doll's houses at Imaginosity.

exhibits are interactive. The stadium tour is a real buzz and the novelty of standing on the pitch in a huge stadium with a capacity of nearly 90,000 gets any spine tingling. The museum enjoyed a major facelift in 2009. ⏲ 1½ hr. See p 17, ❶.

⓬ ★★ Airfield House & Farm. In suburban Dundrum, this gorgeous farm cottage built in the 1820s has been updated as an urban farm, with livestock, ornate gardens, a small museum, and a spacious cafe. There are year-round activities plus opportunities to get up close to the goats, geese, and cows. Inside the grounds, the tiny **Car Museum** has vintage vehicles belonging to two feisty sisters who lived in the house, including a 1923 Peugeot and a 1927 Rolls Royce. ⏲ 2–3 hr. Upper Kilmacud Rd, Dundrum. ☎ 01-298 4301. www.airfield. ie. Admission €6 adults, €3 children 3–18 years, €18 family. Tues–Sat

10am–5pm; Sun & hols 11am–5pm. LUAS: Balally.

⓭ ★★ Imaginosity. Tailor-made for the under 9s, this is a haven of play and make-believe. Let the kids loose in the 'construction company' to build walls with foam bricks, bash the musical pipes, or fill the tiny shopping cart with plastic fruit, fish, and bread and take to the toy check-out. There's even a stage for wannabe stars complete with sound effects, make-up mirrors, and a dressing-up box. Very busy at weekends and school holidays when advance booking is recommended. ⏲ 2 hr. The Plaza, Beacon South Quarter, Sandyford. ☎ 01-217 6130. www.imaginosity.ie. Admission €8.50 adults & children 3–18 years; €7.50 toddlers aged 1–2 & concs; €2 babies 6–12 mth. Mon 1:30–5:30pm; Tues–Fri & hols 9:30am–5:30pm; Sat & Sun 10am–6pm. LUAS: Stillorgan then 10-min walk.

Georgian Dublin

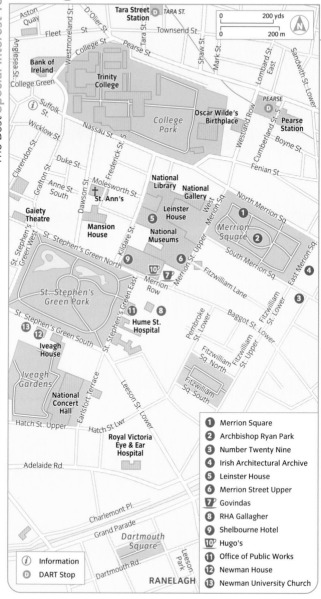

1	Merrion Square
2	Archbishop Ryan Park
3	Number Twenty Nine
4	Irish Architectural Archive
5	Leinster House
6	Merrion Street Upper
7	Govindas
8	RHA Gallagher
9	Shelbourne Hotel
10	Hugo's
11	Office of Public Works
12	Newman House
13	Newman University Church

i Information

D DART Stop

Graceful Georgian architecture has been a Dublin icon ever since flat-fronted five-storey terraces in the 1700s were built for the aristocracy and affluent gentry. Cream of the crop is Merrion Square. START: **Bus 4, 5, 7 & 45 to Merrion Square.**

❶ ★★ **Merrion Square.** The most famous of Dublin's Georgian squares was completed in the late 18th century and has hardly altered since. Blue plaques galore include **Oscar Wilde**'s childhood home at no. 1 (now the American College), **Daniel O'Connell**'s home at no. 58, and **William Butler Yeats** at no. 82. Houses have distinguished fanlights, the semi-circular glass above each doorway, which were more ornate according to the owners' wealth, and doorways typically wide to accommodate the bulky bustles of the lady's Georgian dresses. Doors are characteristically colorful: according to local folklore, after Queen Victoria died and the British painted their doors black for mourning, the Irish painted theirs anything but. ⏱ *45 min. Bus: 7, 10, 45.*

Typical Georgian doorway.

❷ ★ kids **Archbishop Ryan Park.** At the center of Merrion Square, pathways meander around the bijoux green space. Don't miss the sculpture of a slouching **Oscar Wilde** (at the north-west corner), with each color made from a different natural stone. Wearing a Trinity College tie, his expression is half humorous and half serious, conveying both sides of his writing and life. Nearby are a bust of **Michael Collins** and a huge wooden sculpture of a jester's chair dedicated to **Dermot Morgan**, star of the BBC TV series *Father Ted*. ⏱ *45 min.*

❸ ★ kids **Number Twenty Nine.** This small house-museum gives an insight into middle-class family life in Georgian Dublin, with rooms retaining their original 1800s artifacts. Elegant furnishings from the Georgian era and earlier include a handsome long-case clock in the hallway, ornate mahogany chairs, and a portrait of revolutionary Robert Emmet (1778–1803) with a mysterious history. Kids will love the huge dolls' house in the top-floor nursery. ⏱ *1 hr. 29 Fitzwilliam St. Lower.* ☎ *01-702 6165. www.esb.ie/ numbertwentynine/. Admission €6 adults, €3 concs, free children 15 and under. Tues–Sat 10am–5pm, Sun noon–5pm. Closed Mon & hols. Bus: 7, 10, 45.*

❹ ★ **Irish Architectural Archive.** Merrion Square's largest terraced house is one of the few archives with public access. Browse through photos from the 1930s and drawings from the 1700s of houses throughout Ireland to discover their histories (I enjoyed being able to see old photos of my grandparents' house from 1930). Its gallery hosts

Leinster House forms a majestic landmark.

photography exhibitions, often with free lunchtime lectures. ⏱ *45 min. 45 Merrion Square.* ☎ *01-663 3040. www.iarc.ie. Free admission. Tues–Fri 10am–5pm.*

5 ★★ **Leinster House.** Walk up Merrion Square South and peek through the sturdy railings to see the two houses of the National Parliament: the **Dáil** (House of Deputies) and **Seanad** (Senate). Built in 1745 as the town house of the Earl of Kildare, who later became the Duke of Leinster, this is said to be the prototype for the U.S. White House (which was built by Dublin-educated architect James Hoban). At the time, the area was undeveloped and known rather disparagingly as 'the lands of tib and tom'. The Earl was advised against building a town house in the 'country'—however he had the last laugh when, two decades later, this became the most fashionable part of town. Tours of the **Department of the Taoiseach** (Prime Minister) every Saturday grant you privileged access to the PM's office, including family photos and a beautiful Bossi fireplace, plus stained glass and paintings by local artists adorning the walls. ⏱ *tour 40 min.* ☎ *01-619 4000. Free admission. Sat 10:30am–2:15pm; tickets from National Gallery (p 13,* **2** *) from 10am. Meet inside Merrion St. entrance.*

6 ★ **Merrion Street Upper.** From Leinster House you'll pass the National Museum of Natural History (p 29, **4**), and 24 Merrion Street Upper, birthplace of **Arthur Wellesley** better known as the first Duke of Wellington. Born to Anglo-Irish parents, he kept in contact with his Irish friends and family despite becoming one of England's greatest military leaders. When someone pointed out that being born in Dublin made him Irish, he allegedly replied, 'Being born in a stable does not make one a horse'. His home is now part of the elegant Merrion Hotel (p 143), superbly restored and famous for its artwork as well as luxury accommodation. Around the corner on Merrion Row is the tiny **Huguenot Cemetery** (now closed), resting place for French Protestants expelled from France in the 17th century. ⏱ *10 min.*

7 🧒 **Govindas.** Stop for a cheap, filling lunch at this simple Indian vegetarian joint run by Hari Krishnas, but no orange robes here. *18 Merrion Row.* ☎ *01-661 5095. $.*

8 ★★ **RHA Gallagher.** The Royal Hibernian Academy has been an artist-based institution since 1823. This spacious gallery has enjoyed a recent refurbishment including a cafe and bookstore, showcasing contemporary artists mainly from Ireland. ⏱ *45 min. Ely Place.* ☎ *01-661 2558. www.royalhibernianacademy. ie. Free admission. Mon–Sat 11am–7pm; Sun 2–5pm.*

⑨ ★ Shelbourne Hotel. Founded in 1824, Dublin's most celebrated hotel is a Georgian masterpiece which hosted the great and the good in Irish high society, plus visitors like Orson Welles and William Thackeray. Take tea in the lounge to the grand piano's dulcet tunes and think back to the Easter Rising in 1916, when a British machine-gun crew positioned themselves on the fifth floor. Ladies taking tea were urged to move to a back room, advice heeded quickly when a bullet flew through a noble tea-taker's hat and hit a mirror. The hotel was also the venue for the meeting to draft the Irish Constitution in 1922. *See p 145.*

Historic hospitality at The Shelbourne.

⑩ Hugo's. If you're still peckish, this stylish restaurant and wine bar serves a charcuterie or cheese platter. Brunch is also served during weekends until 4pm. *6 Merrion Row.* ☎ *01-676 5955. $$.*

⑪ ★ Office of Public Works. Pop into the foyer of this beautiful Georgian building for the display of Irish marble on its walls. Panels of more than 40 different types show off a rainbow of colors including the mossy green from Connemara, black speckled with white shapes looking like a night sky from Galway, and rust red from Clonony. ⏱ *15 min. 51 St. Stephen's Green.* ☎ *01-647 6000. Free admission. Mon–Thurs 9:15am–5:30pm, Fri 9:15am–5:15pm.*

⑫ ★★ Newman House. This Georgian gem was founded by John Henry Newman in the mid-19th century to form the Catholic University (now UCD). Best known for its exquisite 18th-century stuccowork by the Lafrancini brothers, famous ex-pupils include Jesuit poet Gerard Manley Hopkins and James Joyce (as featured in his *Portrait of the Artist*).

A highlight is the Apollo Room, with plasterwork scenes of Apollo and the nine muses of the arts. Shift your gaze to the magnificent Cuban mahogany staircase as you sweep down; no wonder that the film *Becoming Jane*, depicting the steamy life of Jane Austen, was filmed here. *85–86 St. Stephen's Green.* ☎ *01-716 7422. www.ucd.ie. Entry by tour only. Admission: €6 adults; €4 concs & children 13–17 years; free for 12 & under. June–Aug, Tues–Fri 2pm, 3pm, & 4pm.*

⑬ ★★ Newman University Church. Adjacent to the house (see ⑫), stands the 1850s church that Newman deemed to be essential and so paid for it himself. He was quoted as saying that he intended to 'build a large barn and decorate it in the style of a basilica'. There's certainly a richness of early Italian and Byzantine styles, but don't miss the astounding windows from the bottom of glass bottles and the garishly renovated paintings of the Stations of the Cross. ⏱ *30 min. St. Stephen's Green South. Free admission. Daily 9am–5pm (provisional).*

Trinity College

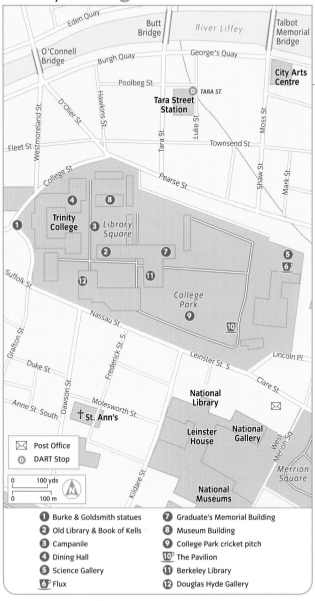

1 Burke & Goldsmith statues
2 Old Library & Book of Kells
3 Campanile
4 Dining Hall
5 Science Gallery
6 Flux

7 Graduate's Memorial Building
8 Museum Building
9 College Park cricket pitch
10 The Pavilion
11 Berkeley Library
12 Douglas Hyde Gallery

Dating back to 1592, Ireland's oldest college has seen great writers and esteemed academics graduate from its hallowed halls—not all of them complimentary: Samuel Beckett allegedly quipped 'Trinity's graduates were like cream: thick and rich.' Established by Queen Elizabeth I, Catholics were forbidden to join unless they accepted the Protestant faith, restrictions only lifted in 1970. START: **Bus 15, 50, & 77 to College St.**

Trinity old boy Oliver Goldsmith.

❶ Burke & Goldsmith statues.

Guarding the Regent House entrance to Trinity are the imposing statues of Edmund Burke and Oliver Goldsmith, cast in white marble by 19th-century sculptor John Henry Foley. Burke (1729–97) became a British statesman thanks to his prowess in political philosophy. Author of *She Stoops to Conquer,* Goldsmith (1728–74) had a colorful life after graduating in theology and law from Trinity; he studied medicine in Edinburgh and traveled through Europe before becoming a noted poet and playwright.

❷ Old Library & Book of Kells.

Inside the grand Old Library, a majestic, huge paneled hall containing more than 200,000 books, visitors line up around the block for this one. The illuminated copy of the *Book of Kells*, four gospels written in Latin around A.D. 800, is lavishly decorated and one of the most famous books in the world. Two volumes are displayed in glass cases and, as part of the complete **Turning Darkness into Light** exhibition, also on display are the *Book of Armagh* and the even older *Book of Durrow*. If, like me, you dislike peering through crowds for a glimpse (I'm too short), try around 1pm when the crowds may have thinned out a little. Even if it's hard to get a proper look at the Book, the view down the length of the Old Library is outstanding. 🕐 *1 hr.*

❸ Campanile.

The most striking and famous monument inside Trinity's grounds, the white Campanile, or bell-tower, grabs your attention as you enter through the main archway. Dating back to the mid-19th century, built by Sir Charles Lanyon,

The Campanile, Trinity's best known landmark.

Trinity College: Practical Matters

Covering a vast 16 hectares (40 acres), this oasis of cobbled, sculpture-filled green lies calmly in the city center. Be prepared for long lines outside the Old Library to see the *Book of Kells*, with occasional temporary closure for visiting foreign dignitaries. In summer, it's worth buying a combined ticket that includes entrance to the *Book of Kells*, plus a guided walk of the college campus led by a student for just an extra couple of euros. Admission to the Old Library: €9 adults, €8 concs, €18 family, free children 11 and under. Monday to Saturday 9:30am to 5pm, Sunday (May–Sept) 9:30am to 4:30pm, (Oct–Apr) noon to 4:30pm. Combined *Book of Kells* and campus tour (mid-May–Sept): €10. Tours: daily every 40 minutes 10:15am to 3.40pm. ☎ 01-896 1000. www.tcd.ie.

it stands on the site of the college's original foundations from 400 years earlier. Walk all the way around and gaze up at its peak—it looks even better in the sunshine.

❹ **Dining Hall.** Here's a real treat in store: the immensely high-ceilinged hall and wooden paneling make even your cup of tea and scone seem special. The building was originally designed by Richard Castle in the 1740s, but after collapsing twice, was rebuilt by Hugh Darley around 1760. Damaged yet again, this time by fire in 1984, it underwent prize-winning restoration. Visitors can pop in for an inexpensive lunch and gaze at the portrait-filled walls.

❺ ★★ **kids Science Gallery.** Opened in 2008, this innovative two-floor gallery brings historic Trinity bang up to date. Inside, well lit through floor-to-ceiling windows, science is made exciting with several interactive exhibitions per year using practical, concrete examples and genuine researchers, from subjects from the coral reefs to human infections. You might find yourself part of genuine research about

music and the body, or join a discussion about a hot topic. Older kids will love the *Science Safari*, a themed walking tour through Trinity which they can download in advance. 🕐 *45 min.* ☎ *01-896 4107. www.sciencegallery.com. Free admission. Daily 8am–5pm; exhibs Tues–Fri noon–8pm; Sat & Sun noon–6pm.*

❻ ★ **Flux.** Inside the Science Gallery, refresh yourself with Italian cuisine or just a cappuccino, with early-evening aperitivos every Friday. A relaxed and stylish venue. *Trinity College.* ☎ *01-896 1000. $.*

❼ **Graduates' Memorial Building.** The GMB now houses student accommodation—streets ahead of the sort I had to endure—and is also home to the university's history and philosophical societies. The neo-Gothic Victorian building was designed by Sir Thomas Drew in 1892, one of 19th-century Ireland's most distinguished architects. It's not possible to enter, but walk around the outside for a closer look at some of the detailed stonework.

8 Museum Building. Home to the geography and geology departments, this is one of my favorite Dublin hidden gems. Designed by architects Dean and Woodward, with stonemasonry by the famed O'Shea brothers, this mid-19th century creation has intriguing Byzantine and Moorish influences. Samuel Haughton, inventor of the 'humane hangman's drop' was Professor here in the late 19th century. Enter through the main door past two enormous skeletons of giant Irish deer, and check out the domed ceiling and green marbled banisters. The top floor's tiny **Geology Museum** is a must for fans of meteorites, fossils, and early amphibians, where the friendly curator is happy to allow visitors to look around. Scenes from the British 1985 film *Educating Rita* were shot here. *Geology Museum.* ☎ *01-896 1477. Free admission. Mon–Fri 10am–5pm.*

9 College Park cricket pitch. As a cricket fan, it's always a pleasure to see a match at the Dublin University Cricket Club, stalwart of Irish cricket for nearly 200 years and played here since the 1820s. Most matches take place during summer weekends (May to early September), and on sunny days students and locals sprawl out on the grass around the boundary. It's fair to say that few follow every ball being bowled, although since Ireland shocked the world by beating Pakistan in the 2007 Cricket World Cup, interest in the sport has grown.

10 ★ The Pavilion. At the eastern end of the cricket pitch is 'the Pav', a cafe-bar with balcony. At weekends during a cricket match beer might run out quickly, so be quick to stock up. ☎ *01-896 1000. $.*

11 Berkeley Library. Some love its appearance, most hate it (including me), but the library located between two architectural masterpieces has sure caused controversy since day one. Designed by Paul Koralek, it honors Bishop George Berkeley, famed for his philosophical theory of 'immaterialism' (things that can't be proved cannot exist), which went against the theories of Sir Isaac Newton and the Catholic Church. A university was eventually set up in California in his name (in the USA it's pronounced 'Barkeley'). Arnaldo Pomodoro's gleaming golden sculpture **Sphere within a Sphere** (1983) stands outside the library.

12 Douglas Hyde Gallery. Housed in the 1970s-**Arts Building**, this gallery houses temporary exhibitions in two rooms. It includes work from top contemporary artists from Ireland and overseas, usually in a variety of media. It's usually very quiet, and definitely worth a look. ⏱ *30 min.* ☎ *01-896 1116. www. douglashydegallery.com. Free admission. Mon–Fri 11am–6pm; Thurs 11am–7pm; Sat 11am–4:45pm.*

Berkeley Library.

Vikings & Medieval Dubh Linn

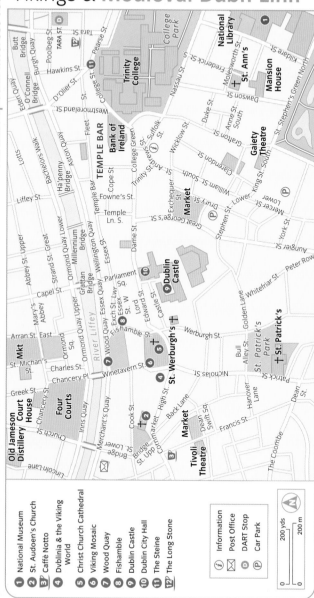

1 National Museum
2 St. Audoen's Church
3 Caffé Notto
4 Dvblinia & the Viking World
5 Christ Church Cathedral
6 Viking Mosaic
7 Wood Quay
8 Fishamble
9 Dublin Castle
10 Dublin City Hall
11 The Steine
12 The Long Stone

ⓘ Information
⊠ Post Office
Ⓞ DART Stop
Ⓟ Car Park

0 — 200 yds
0 — 200 m

Visitors come to see Dublin's literary and political history, yet its Viking past is lesser known. When two fleets of Norsemen arrived on the Liffey in A.D. 837 and established camp, near today's Dublin Castle, they named it An Dubh Linn (literally Black Pool). This tour shows off some of the fascinating remains of that era, especially around Temple Bar, Wood Quay, and Dublin Castle

START: **Bus 7, 10, 11, & 13 to Merrion Row.**

1 ★★ National Museum. This well laid-out museum certainly knows how to pack archaeological eras into a small area. Its Viking section includes relics discovered in the 1960s' and 1970s' excavations at Wood Quay (p 42, **7**). Exhibits include domestic artifacts, well-furnished female graves, and even weighing scales proving there was more to the Vikings than being warriors and marauding raiders; they were also traders who made Dublin a good base. From cemeteries unearthed in the Dublin areas of Kilmainham and Islandbridge—the largest outside Scandinavia—you'll see the skeletal remains and weapons they were buried with. Public tours 11:30am and 3pm daily. ⏱ 1½ hr. Kildare St. ☎ 01-677 7444. www.museum.ie. Free admission. Tues–Sat 10am–5pm; Sun 2–5pm. Guided tours €2 (15 and under free). Tues–Sat 3:30pm & Sun 2:30pm. Bus: 7, 8, 10, 11.

2 ★★ St. Audoen's Church. Dublin's only remaining medieval parish church is located on what was once its principal street, and completed in 1212—although a grave slab 300 years older indicates that an earlier church occupied the same site. The exhibition inside the Visitors' Centre illustrates the area during medieval times, then the city's commercial heart. The church itself is more impressive (staff are happy to show you around). Look out for the 1190 baptismal font and the funerary tomb of a 1620 Alderman, decorated with skull and crossbones and so proving that it didn't always symbolize poison or

The Portlester Tomb at St. Audoen's Church.

pirates. In the tower, the 15th-century Portlester tomb has effigies of Baron Portlester and his wife Margaret looking exceedingly restful. Sunday services (Church of Ireland) are open to everyone, a perfect opportunity to hear Ireland's oldest bells, dating back to 1423. Opposite the main reception desk, I love the postcards of various tradesmen of the time, telling stories of their lives. ⏲ *45 min. Cornmarket, High St.* ☎ *01-677 0088.* www. heritageireland.ie. *Free admission. Daily Jun–Sept, 9:30am–5:30pm.*

3 ★ **Caffé Noto.** Serving coffee, sandwiches, and smoothies in relaxed surroundings (the former bank has retained the interior brick walls, now covered with art from local students), peruse the daily papers or watch the busy Cornmarket outside. *79 Thomas St.* ☎ *01-454 7223. $*

4 ★ **kids Dvblinia & the Viking World.** One especially for kids (see p 29, **8**), the heritage center is aptly built at Dublin's medieval heart, illustrating local life since Strongbow and his knights captured the city in 1170.

The Crypt at Christ Church Cathedral.

Enter through the reconstructed Viking ship to Viking World with markets, burials, and even a slave auction. The History Hunters exhibition shows off artifacts from the Wood Quay (see p 42) excavations, including the skeleton of a 12th-century Hiberno-Norse woman—probably your only chance to look a 900-year-old Dubliner in the eye. ⏲ *1 hr. See p 29,* **8**.

5 ★ **kids Christ Church Cathedral.** Originally a wooden structure founded by the 11th-century Norse King Sitric, the cathedral was replaced by a stone building and then, 700 years later, restored. Inside, look out for Strongbow's tomb, and the original 13th-century ornate floor tiles. Descend to the medieval crypt, extending under the entire cathedral and dating back to the 11th century, making it Dublin's oldest structure. If you peep through the glass in the floor, you can see its 11th-century foundations, later demolished by the Anglo-Normans. There's also a taste of punishment, medieval style, with a pair of 17th-century stocks, which were originally in the churchyard. ⏲ *1 hr. See p 15,* **9**.

6 Viking Mosaic. Adjacent to Christ Church Cathedral, at the southern end of Winetavern Street, look down at the pavement. In dark stone, you'll see the full-sized plan of a typical early Viking building site. While you're in the vicinity, look out for bronze slabs in the pavement, including one outside the main entrance to Christ Church Cathedral, indicating the locations of artifacts excavated. You can see the real things in the National Museum (see p 9, **7**). *Winetavern St.*

7 ★ **kids Wood Quay.** Scene of the city's most controversial construction: as Dublin Corporation started building their new HQ here

The site of the original 'black pool' can be found in the garden of Dublin Castle.

in the 1970s, preserved remains of the Viking city and medieval city walls were unearthed to reveal one of Europe's most important Viking sites. When the council showed no intention of changing their plans, locals protested en masse and after court cases, massive public campaigns—known as the Battle of Wood Quay—and further excavations, building plans were altered, leaving the remains of the city walls piled up in the basement and Viking relics in the National Museum (p 9, **7**). The site was built over in the 1990s when the last phase of the construction was completed. Inside, the new **My City** interactive exhibition also houses the City Wall Space, featuring the original Hiberno Viking city wall dating from A.D. 11. Outside the office, the Viking ship sculpture by Betty Maguire is a symbolic representation of the era. *Viking ship by Wood Quay, between O'Donovan Rossa and Grattan bridges.*

8 ★ **Fishamble.** Now filled with modern-day hedonistic temples of pleasure and culture (pubs and clubs), this was the hub of medieval Dublin, and a few relics remain. Fishamble, the oldest street, was the original location of the fish market. Look out for the plaque on the wall

next to the **George Frederic Handel Hotel** (no. 16–18), marking the spot of the former 'Musick Hall'; this was the venue of the world's first performance of **Handel's *Messiah***—which he also conducted—on 13th April, 1742. Look for the Turk's Head bar on Essex

Viking landmark in the midst of traffic.

Gate—outside that and the Czech Inn (formerly Isolde's Tower) opposite are two stone pillars marking the original city gates.

⑨ ★★ Dublin Castle. The tour of the castle interior gives a flavor of the high life of royalty and the political elite. But the exterior has an older history. Several years after 60 Viking warships sailed up the Liffey in A.D. 837, the castle was the site of a high-ridged fort. After the Irish expelled them, the Norsemen returned and settled just west of the castle, building up a town called Dyflinn with the King's palace on the site of the castle. The site of the original 'black pool' (from where the name Dyflinn and later Dubh Linn originate) is the circular garden behind the castle with Celtic design. If you take the castle tour, you'll visit the Undercroft, where parts of the town defenses and settlements can be seen. ⏲ *1 hr. See p 14,* **⑥**.

⑩ ★ Dublin City Hall. If you haven't yet ventured beyond the City Hall's atrium, explore the **Story of the Capital** exhibition, offering a decent insight into Viking Dublin, and fascinating medieval relics. Look out for the original 13th-century City Seal, made from two bronze moulds, which were filled with hot, red liquid wax and sealed onto legal documents. There is also the earliest Norman document in Ireland, dating back to 1171. (See also p 10, **⑩**). ⏲ *30 min. Cork Hill, Dame St.* ☎ *01-222 2204. www.dublincity.ie. Mon–Sat 10am–5:15pm, Sun 2–5pm. Free admission to Rotunda. Exhibition: €4 adults, €2 students, €1.50 children 15 and under. Bus: 56A, 77, 123.*

⑪ ★ The Steine. Traffic whizzes around one of Dublin's busiest roundabouts, yet its center marks where the Vikings first landed. The Steine, a granite slab, represents the original Standing Stones, 360–420cm (12–14 ft) high, that the Vikings erected in the 10th or 11th centuries to mark the boundaries of their Dublin territories. This one is a reproduction, carved by Cliodna Cussen, depicting the faces of Ivor, the 9th-century Viking King of Dublin. In front is the **Townsend Street police station**, once the headquarters of the Garda and where Michael Collins entered secretly during the 1916 uprising to take a peek at the records. *Junction of D'Olier, Townsend & College Streets.*

⑫ ★★ The Long Stone. With timber window-frames, stained-glass skylight, and carved wooden ceiling, this pub's theme fits into the area's history. Resembling a medieval museum, its centerpiece is the fireplace surround—a sculpture of Balder, the Viking god of light and warmth. Get back to practical matters; have a drink, with excellent food served all day. *10 Townsend St.* ☎ *01-671 8102. $.* ●

The Long Stone's distinctive fireplace.

JIM
LARKIN

North of **Royal Canal**

1. National Botanic Gardens
2. Tea Room
3. Our Lady of Dolores
4. Watchtower
5. Glasnevin Cemetery
6. Kavanagh's
7. Royal Canal
8. Brendan Behan sculpture
9. Croke Park
10. Mountjoy Square

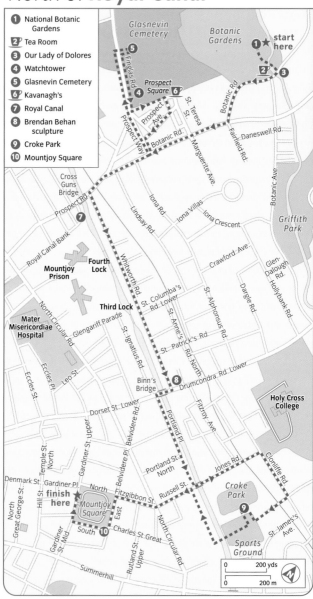

Previous page: Larkin statue.

The letter O off the beaten track, this walk takes in some of my Dublin favorites, including gardens, heroic history, and sporting prowess. Try to save it for a fine day as it covers a large distance with few sheltering spots. Although these days the Northside is relatively unfashionable, you'll come across one of the city's first prestigious Georgian squares. START: **Bus 13, 13A & 19 to Botanic Gardens.**

There are over 8,400 panes of glass in the curvilinear wall.

❶ ★★★ kids National Botanic Gardens.

Going strong for more than 200 years, these 20-hectare (50-acre) gardens house more than 20,000 species of rare and cultivated plants from around the world. Depending on the season, you might see rhododendrons, roses, vast conifers, or Chinese plants. The curvilinear wall is a real highlight: an immense glass house whose walls comprise more than 8,400 panes of glass (imagine cleaning that lot).The palm house opposite is also stunning—amazing that it arrived as a flat-pack from Scotland. Regular exhibitions and talks take place in the Visitor Centre. ⏱ 1½ hr. Botanic Rd, Glasnevin. ☎ 01-804 0300. www.botanicgardens.ie. Free admission. Daily 9am–6pm summer (mid-Feb to mid-Nov); daily 9am–4:30pm winter. Free tours Sun noon & 2:30pm.

❷ kids Tea Room.
The Visitor Centre's cafe is great for resting weary feet (or drying off). Refuel with hot drinks and snacks, or hot meals like jacket potatoes at lunchtime. *National Botanic Gardens.* ☎ 01-857 0909. $.

❸ ★ Our Lady of Dolores.
From a distance it looks like an ebony pyramid in the middle of a roundabout, which is pretty much what it is. Constructed from dark timber, the **Pyramid Church** (its unofficial name) was built in 1972. Although the interior lacks ornate charm, etched glass windows depict the 14 Stations of the Cross (the final hours of Jesus before his crucifixion), making an interesting perusal. ⏱ 15 min. Cnr Botanic Ave & Botanic Rd. ☎ 01-837 9445. Free admission. Daily 9am–6:30pm; Mass Sun 10am & 11:30am, 6:30pm.

4 ★★★ **Watchtower.** As you walk around the cemetery's perimeter wall, you'll pass the watchtower on the southwest corner. Here, watchmen would guard against the bodysnatchers, or 'sack-em-ups', who attempted to dig up fresh corpses to supply the medical profession for anatomy students. *Finglas Rd.*

5 ★★★ **Glasnevin Cemetery.** The cemetery brings the nation's history, ironically, to life. This vast burial ground, Ireland's largest, opened its gates in 1832 after Daniel O'Connell's efforts to allow Catholics the first chance to be buried in their own cemetery. Before that, the wealthy were buried in Protestant graveyards; the poor by the roadside. An estimated 1.5 million people lie here, half of them in unmarked graves. As well as ordinary people, luminaries from Ireland's history interred here include **Daniel**

Ornate Celtic crosses at Glasnevin Cemetery.

O'Connell (see p 25, **11**) in a recently repainted crypt decorated with Celtic art; **Michael Collins**, whose grave is always covered with fresh flowers; **Charles Stuart Parnell** (see p 24, **6**), marked by a huge stone; former president **Eamon de Valera**, whose gravestone is often vandalized; and **Bobby Sands** and the IRA hunger-strikers of the 1980s. Admire the stonework and ornate crosses as you pick your way through the rows. The daily tours by local historians are unmissable. From early 2010, the **Museum and Heritage Centre** near the entrance will give an interactive illuminating history of the cemetery and gravediggers, plus a camera obscura posted on top of Daniel O'Connell's crypt. ⏱ 1½ hr. *Glasnevin Rd.* ☎ 01-830 1133. *www. glasnevintrust.ie. Free admission. Daily 8am–6pm; tours daily 2:30pm, €5, children under 16 free.*

6 ★ **Kavanagh's.** Best known by locals as The Gravedigger's, this friendly pub's location next to the cemetery meant 'popping in' before a funeral, resulting in corpses, allegedly, left forgotten on the roadside. Tasty tapas and Italian breads are served lunchtimes and early evenings. This friendly suburban pub has been run by the same family since 1833. *1 Prospect Square.* ☎ 01-830 7978. $.

7 ★ **Royal Canal.** Join the canal from Prospect Rd for a serene walk along its bank. Several locks along the way, still hand-operated, date back to the 1790s and there's usually a fair smattering of ducks and the occasional swan. Peer over the high wall on your right to catch a glimpse of the infamous **Mountjoy Prison,** where Brendan Behan did time (see **8**). The canal's western

The Royal Canal with Croke Park in the background.

stretch is currently being restored and will take many more years to complete, including bridges to be replaced with higher ones so boats can pass under. It gets more untouched as you head west from this point but, should you fancy the walk, stick to daylight hours. ⏱ *45 min to include Croke Park* ⑨.

⑧ ★★ **Brendan Behan sculpture.** Of Dublin's countless statues, sculptures, and busts of famous characters, this is my favorite. Unveiled in 2003 on the 80th anniversary of Behan's birth, it commemorates the author of *Borstal Boy* (among other books), who was notorious not only as a great writer, but also a revolutionary and immense drinker. The former earned him a spell in Mountjoy Prison (caught smuggling explosives to England), the latter an early grave (he died at the age of 41) and many tales of his fondness for the bottle. Now, he sits on the bench talking to a pigeon and for a former hell-raiser, this peaceful setting makes me smile as I sit down next to him. After

you pass the sculpture, cross Drumcondra Rd and join the canal on its opposite bank.

⑨ ★ **Croke Park.** It's hard to miss the mammoth stadium as you continue east along the canal. Even if you've already visited the **GAA Museum** and taken the stadium tour, it's worth noting the amazing history of this sporting venue. Built by volunteers to promote Gaelic games, starting with initial meetings in 1884, Croke Park has played a major part in Irish nationalist history as host to Gaelic football and hurling for over a century. Its founding members would have probably turned in their graves on realizing that, after much discussion and government funding, it hosted international football (soccer) and rugby matches from 2007–10 while Lansdowne Road stadium underwent redevelopment. Enter the museum for an interesting (free) display on the GAA's history, which celebrated its 125th anniversary in 2009. *See p 17,* ①.

⑩ **Mountjoy Square.** Although now rather shabby and off the beaten track, this area was the epitome of fashionable Dublin until well into the 19th century. Originally known as Gardiner's Square, after its founder Luke Gardiner, building began in 1792 in typical Georgian style: 18 houses on each side of a uniform square. Today, much of it has been converted into flats and decline has set in. The south side of the square has altered the most, although the eastern side retains much of its original charm. Former residents include the great stuccodore Charles Thorpe (nos. 12 and 22), who worked on City Hall, and the writer Sean O'Casey, who rented a room at no. 35. From here, it's a 20-minute walk along Gardiner Place to reach O'Connell Street.

Renewed **Docklands**

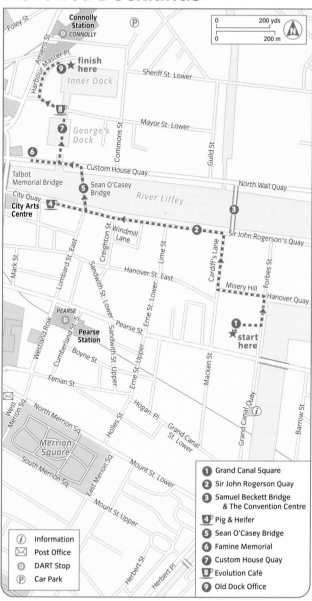

1	Grand Canal Square
2	Sir John Rogerson Quay
3	Samuel Beckett Bridge & The Convention Centre
4	Pig & Heifer
5	Sean O'Casey Bridge
6	Famine Memorial
7	Custom House Quay
8	Evolution Café
9	Old Dock Office

ⓘ	Information
⊠	Post Office
Ⓓ	DART Stop
Ⓟ	Car Park

ublin's mammoth regeneration project sees cranes and pile drivers galore, changing the once no-go area into the slick Docklands. Now filled with glass-fronted apartments and wine bars, the city's focal point is shifting farther east although, as of recently, many lie empty. You might prefer to explore the area during the slightly busier weekdays. START: **Bus 2, 3 & 77. DART: Grand Canal Dock.**

① ★★ **Grand Canal Square.** The city's largest paved public square is a good point to observe the docks and the surfeit of rebuilding in the area. Designed by top U.S. architect Martha Schwartz, the garden and concourse opened in 2007 with red paved walkways, giant red rods (reminding me of glowing chopsticks), a water feature, and plants. (Hint: Come back at night to see the 'chopsticks' lit up and the gorgeous reflections on the still water.) On the west side of the square, the new **Grand Canal Theatre,** designed by Daniel Libeskind, is due to open in 2010, along with a luxury hotel, apartments, and restaurants. **Surfdock,** located in an old Aran Islands Ferry on the docks' south side (accessed from Pearse St.) offers taster windsurfing sessions for adults within the docks. *Surfdock.* ☎ *01-667 0988. www. surfdock.ie. www.grandcanal square.ie.*

Grand Canal's 'chopsticks'.

② ★ **kids Sir John Rogerson Quay.** The life-size iron sculpture *The Linesman* by Dony MacManus

The Linesman on the Liffey.

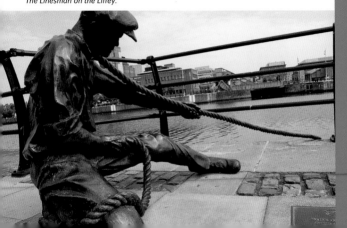

depicts a docker heaving in ropes, dragging something presumably extremely heavy given the look on his face. The quay, developed in 1713 by former MP Sir John Rogerson is also the location for the DDDA offices (Dublin Docklands Development Agency) which has masterminded the docklands development.

③ ★ **Samuel Beckett Bridge & The Convention Centre.** Santiago Calatrava's dramatic design, likened to a harp lying on its side, dominates the area and is the latest bridge to cross the Liffey. With four traffic lanes, cycle tracks, and footpaths, it also opens at 90 degrees to enable ships to pass. It leads directly to The Convention Centre, a purpose-built international conference venue, which even the keenest architectural connoisseurs would liken to a slanted baked bean tin. It's due to open fully in September 2010. *Spencer Dock.*

④ ★ kids **Pig & Heifer.** New York deli style comes to Dublin. Fill up on pastrami on rye, take your pick from the fresh salad bar, or try pasta and pizzas in the evening. *21–23 City Quay.* ☎ *01-633 6972. www.pig andheifer.ie. $.*

⑤ ★ **Sean O'Casey Bridge.** Honoring the great Dublin writer (1880–1964), this is the third bridge built over the Liffey since 2000. As you cross the 100m (110 yd) over the river, mutter to yourself, 'The whole world is in a terrible state of chassis', from O'Casey's *Juno and the Paycock.* Feel the bridge's slight sway, no doubt prompting the nickname Quiver on the River from locals (which also relates to the Millennium or Mill Bridge, farther down the river). The graceful construction opens into two sections, swinging 90 degrees to allow tall boats to pass through.

⑥ ★★ kids **Famine Memorial.** This striking bronze series of sculptures commemorates the Great Famine of the mid-19th century, when Ireland lost millions of people due to starvation and emigration. It's fitting

The striking Famine Memorial.

The Old Dock Offices, now a comfortable bar and restaurant.

that it stands here, on the very docks where many desperate people left on U.S.-bound ships seeking work and survival. The memorial, created by Rowan Gillespie, was allegedly commissioned for Boston, Massachusetts, but their local mayor found it 'too depressing', hence it stayed right here. Depicting several hunger-ravaged people, plus a dog, the haunting image stands ironically in the shadow of the **International Financial Services Centre (IFSC)**, created by the government in 1987. The symbolism is harsh (intentionally?) given that this is the engine room of the modern Irish economy containing half the world's top 50 banks—even taking into account the recent global recession. Amazing what changes occur in 150 years. *Custom House Quay. www.ifsc.ie.*

7 ★★ **Custom House Quay.** Located in George's Dock, **the chq building**, recently renovated into a chic shopping center, has a fascinating history. Constructed in 1796 and designed by John Rennie, this was

previously known as Stack A, built as a warehouse storing tobacco and tea, with vaults for wine, rum, and whiskey. On an unforgettable night in 1833, a devastating fire caused burning spirits to flow into the river, and it was noted that 'the Liffey was a sheet of flame for half its breadth', visible for miles (and doubtless there would have been many 'what a waste' comments flying round that night). In 1856 it hosted the famous Crimean War Banquet to honor Irish troops who served in a war that suffered a total of 750,000 casualties. In the mall (often deserted) that lies there today, you can still see the original elements of the roof. *Docklands. www.chq.ie. Mon–Fri 7am–7pm; Sat 10am–6pm; Sun noon–6pm.*

8 ★★ kids **Evolution Café.** Within IFSC territory (so lots of city types getting takeouts), this branch of O'Brien's has a tiny balcony overlooking George's Dock. Even if you're not hungry, have a coffee, take a seat on the balcony, and enjoy the view. *3 George's Dock, IFSC.* ☎ *01-670 1900. Mon–Fri. $.*

9 ★ **Old Dock Office.** The old offices, nestled in Custom House Dock, have been beautifully restored and now house the Harbourmaster Bar and Restaurant. It's great to see buildings like this: well preserved, respecting its past, and transformed into something functional that people can enjoy. Dubliners also seem to like it; even those resenting the great swathes of Docklands rebuilding that could take the old character away. Return later in the evening for dinner. *Harbourmaster Bar and Restaurant, see p 106.*

The Best Neighborhood Walks

Liffey **Boardwalk**

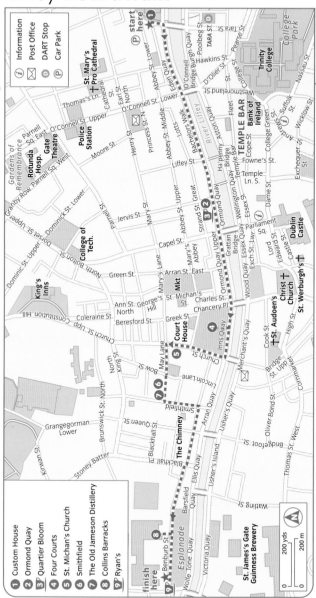

Key:
- ⓘ Information
- ⊠ Post Office
- Ⓓ DART Stop
- Ⓟ Car Park

1 Custom House
2 Ormond Quay
3 Quartier Bloom
4 Four Courts
5 St. Michan's Church
6 Smithfield
7 The Old Jameson Distillery
8 Collins Barracks
9 Ryan's

Created as part of a Millennium project, the Liffey Boardwalk is a good starting point to explore the river's traffic-free north bank. Even considering the city's high rainfall, it's no surprise that the river has never flooded, given the immensely high river wall built in 1800. We start with the imposing historic landmark Custom House, ending at one of the city's finest museums. START: Bus 53A to Custom House Quay or 15, 45 & 65 to Eden Quay. LUAS: Busáras.

1 ★★ Custom House. You'll be hard pushed to miss this glorious building, dominating the north quay and architecturally one of Dublin's most important buildings. Designed by Englishman James Gandon and created in 1791, its exterior is richly adorned with sculptures with strong Irish themes. Take a good look at Hibernia seen embracing Britannia while Neptune drives away famine and despair. It was located on this part of the quay in an attempt to shift the city's center slightly farther east, which angered city merchants at the time. Gaze at this scene at night from the south side of the river, or get up close from around the back through the car park. Ignore signs directing you to a Visitors' Centre—there isn't one!

Sunset on Custom House.

2 ★ Ormond Quay. Walking west along the Boardwalk, you'll come to the loveliest example of recent developments in the area. Walk past the famous Ha'penny Bridge (p 19, **7**), and the **Hags with the Bags** sculpture—two ladies resting on a bench complete with Arnotts shopping bags. You'll then come to the quaint Italian quarter, **Quartier Bloom,** a tiny enclave of eateries with outdoor tables nestled around a cozy alleyway, complete with a huge mural of The Last Supper on the outside wall. It adds a Mediterranean ambience to the place, where locals love to pop in for lunch, a coffee, or to stock up on Italian foodstuffs.

3 ★★ kids Quartier Bloom. For a coffee break, lunch, or ice cream, find a spot in this Italian Quarter and dine alfresco. It's popular on sunny days so choose your venue, pull up a chair, order a latte, and get feasting. *Assorted venues, Lower Ormond Quay. $–$$.*

4 ★★ Four Courts. A Dublin landmark with its large drum-shaped roof topped by a shallow dome, this building originally held the four divisions that made up the judicial system. Designed by James Gandon (see also **1**), its imposing exterior is enhanced by Edward Smyth's sculptures, with Moses flanked by Justice and Mercy on the main pediment. Destroyed by fire during the Civil War of 1921, the building was restored with few changes to the exterior.

The Four Courts, designed by James Gandon.

⑤ ★★ kids St. Michan's Church. Around the corner, St. Michan's is the oldest parish church on the Northside, dating back to 1095 when it served the Viking community. Pop in to see the original organ on which (legend has it) Handel practiced for his first performance of the *Messiah.* Also on show is the original 1720s piece of carved oak depicting 17 musical instruments, which for many years adorned the back of the Irish £50 note. Descend the steep stone steps for a guided tour of the vaults, containing mummified bodies and a couple of skulls, and the remains of barrister brothers John and Henry Sheares, executed for their part in the 1798 Irish rebellion. Bram Stoker could well have been inspired to write *Dracula* from a visit to the vaults with his family. Some years ago it may well have been possible to shake the hands of the corpse (as my cousin claims) but these days it's strictly hands off. ⏱ *20 min. Church St.* ☎ *01-872 4154. Free admission. Tours: €3.50 adults, €3 concs, €2.50 children 14–16 years; free for 12 & under. Mar–Oct: Mon–Fri 10am–12:30pm & 2–4:30pm; Sat 10am–12:30pm. Nov–Feb: Mon–Fri 12:30–3:30pm, Sat 10am–12:30pm.*

⑥ ★ Smithfield. From the church, turn left and cut through May Lane to the recently developed stylish apartments, which some locals love and some hate. Smithfield is the original wide cobbled street where horses and cattle have traded since 1664. The traditional **Horse Market**, Europe's largest, still takes place here on the first Sunday of the month, attracting travelers and villagers from all over Ireland. The rest of the month it's a peaceful urban retreat with newly built studio flats (although many of them appear to be empty) and tasteful street lighting. It also hosts the occasional concert, Christmas market, and ice-rink in winter. On the southern corner you'll see the red-brick 56m-high (183 ft) **Chimney Viewing Tower** with panoramic city views from the top, but at the time of writing this remains closed. *LUAS: Smithfield.*

The Chimney Viewing Tower in Smithfield.

Dublin's three National Museums and is well worth a visit. Built on the site of the neoclassical barracks named after Michael Collins, it opened as a museum in 1997 and includes one of the world's largest collections of Irish silver, the Lord Chancellor's Mace, costumed soldiers, and weaponry. There's also a new permanent exhibition devoted to **John Count McCormack** (1884–1945), the Dublin-born tenor. Save time for *What's In Store,* my personal favorite, a visible storage display cabinet with an astounding 16,000 relics from the National Museums' collection including Indian ceremonial art, Japanese Samurai, and Persian miniatures. Get a coffee from the cafe and take a seat in the vast courtyard. On your way out, look out for Ireland's oldest letter box. 🕐 *1½ hr. Collins Barracks, Benburb St. 🕿 01-677 7444. www.museum.ie. Free admission. Tues–Sat 10am–5pm; Sun 2–5pm. Tours: daily 3pm, €2. LUAS; Museum.*

57 Liffey Boardwalk

Collins Barracks, now the National Museum.

7 ★ kids The Old Jameson Distillery. Well established on the tourist trail, a guided tour of the distillery gives a crash course in the making of the 'water of life' (whiskey), and a potted history since the company was set up in 1780 by John Jameson—a Scot, no less. The tour shows off the huge casks, a model of the cat used to catch mice, and a description of distilling methods. If you fancy taking part in the taste test (to distinguish the difference between Scotch, American, and Irish whiskeys), make sure you volunteer at the beginning of the tour. A complimentary drink is served in the bar afterwards. At the main entrance, check out the original fermentation vats, now visible through a glass section of the floor. *Bow St, Smithfield. 🕿 01-807 2355. www.jamesonwhiskey.com. Admission €13.50 adults, €11 concs, €8 children under 17 years; €30 family (2 adults & 3 children). Daily 9am–6:30pm. Regular tours approx 10am–5:15pm.*

8 ★★★ kids Collins Barracks. Housing the **Museum of Decorative Arts and History**, this is one of

9 ★ Ryan's. Built in 1896 this is one of Dublin's oldest pubs, with original Victorian fittings and mahogany interior. Have a cozy pint or steak, and remember that JFK, Bill Clinton, and George Bush Sr also drank here. *28 Parkgate St. 🕿 01-677 6097. $–$$.*

A painted cart at the Jameson Distillery.

Around **Grafton Street**

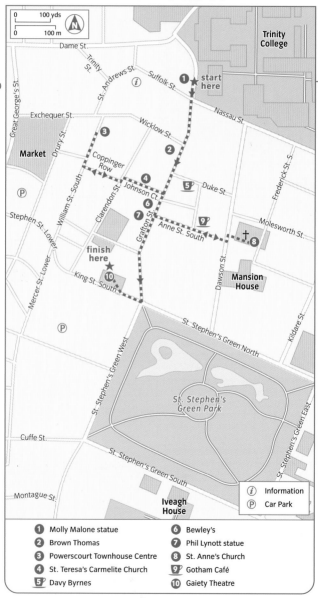

1. Molly Malone statue
2. Brown Thomas
3. Powerscourt Townhouse Centre
4. St. Teresa's Carmelite Church
5. Davy Byrnes
6. Bewley's
7. Phil Lynott statue
8. St. Anne's Church
9. Gotham Café
10. Gaiety Theatre

Dublin's busiest shopping street has been rocking ever since Bewley's and Switzers began trading in the early 1900s, and it's still a shopping hub. Named after the first Duke of Grafton, illegitimate son of Charles II, the balance has shifted over the years from independent Irish stores to predictable U.K. chains, but the architectural detail on the facades still dazzles. START: **Bus 15, 15a, 50 & 77 to College Street.**

Molly Malone with her wares on show.

❶ ★ kids Molly Malone statue. At the northern end of Grafton Street, tourists gather for their photos next to **Jeanne Rynhart**'s statue, probably with an old Irishman playing the penny whistle; a clichéd image of Dublin that storytellers and even historians adore. Molly Malone, known lovingly as the Tart with the Cart, allegedly died of a fever in the 17th century, and her ghost is still said to push her wheelbarrow 'selling Cockles and Mussels alive alive-o' along Grafton Street. But legend has it that her daytime work selling Dublin Bay shellfish was not quite as lucrative as her night-time job as a lady of the night, when she trawled the streets for clients. Some say that Ms Malone really existed, attempting to prove that she was a God-fearing, church-going girl. Most are content with the fairytale, the song (written by a Scotsman), and the tarty

cleavage-revealing statue of the Dish with the Fish.

❷ ★ Brown Thomas. Haberdashers and drapers Hugh Brown and James Thomas opened the doors to Dublin's *grande dame* of style on Grafton Street in 1859. Since then it has grown in stature, moved across the road, nearly gone bankrupt, and merged with Switzers, another long-established store. It's now firmly on the fashionista trail, crammed with international designer gear and the only store on the street to have a dapper top-hat wearing concierge. Brown Thomas oozes style, yet thankfully there's nothing snooty about its manner. *See p 78.*

❸ Powerscourt Townhouse Centre. Cut down Wicklow Street to this popular and stylish shopping mall. This is one of Dublin's finest town mansions, built in the 1770s as a town house and office for Lord Powerscourt, and made from granite mined from his estate in Co. Wicklow. It's fitting that the center today is home to many contemporary boutiques, the Design Centre, and Antique Gallery, as Powerscourt himself was a stylish gent, wearing Parisian fashions and being something of a trend-setter. Enter through the majestic mahogany staircase on Drury Street, with Rococo plasterwork adorning the ceiling. Returning to Grafton Street, cut through the jewelry alleyway, **Johnson Court**. *See p 84.*

④ ★ **St. Teresa's Carmelite Church.** Tucked away down a small alleyway off Grafton Street, this church suddenly seems large on entering and it's certainly an oasis in the midst of shopping frenzy. This was the first Catholic church to be legally built and opened in Dublin, following the 1793 Catholic Relief Act. Marble walls of brown and cream hues greet worshippers, with ornate stained-glass windows designed by Phyllis Burke. *Clarendon St. www.clarendonstreet.com.*

⑤ 📷 **Davy Byrnes.** This is where Leopold Bloom, hero of James Joyce's Ulysses, enjoyed a glass of Burgundy and a Gorgonzola sandwich. If that doesn't take your fancy, you can have an Irish breakfast at an outside table. *21 Duke St.* 📞 *01-677 5217. $.*

⑥ ★★ **Bewley's.** This longstanding Grafton Street landmark is famous for its coffee, and is Ireland's only cafe to hand-roast coffee on the premises. For many of us it's a convenient meeting-place inside and out, but the building also has an interesting history. Built originally as a private residence, in 1758 it was a

boarding preparatory school for sons of VIPs, including the future Duke of Wellington and orator Robert Emmet. The Bewley family, who were Quakers from France, became the country's first tea merchants in 1833; they opened Bewley's Oriental Café as a coffee house in 1927, and furnished it with rich mahogany, brass, and chandeliers, inspired by Parisian and Viennese cafes. Go to the back of the first-floor restaurant (Café Bar Deli, p 102) to see six specially commissioned stained-glass windows by Harry Clarke, with Joshua Bewley's will exhibited next to the windows. The Café Theatre (p 133) upstairs has lunchtime performances and the occasional evening of comedy, drama, or jazz. Or simply go there for its coffee. At the entrance to the second floor, look out for the framed marriage certificate of Ernest Bewley. *78/79 Grafton St.* 📞 *01-672 7720. www.bewleys.com.*

⑦ ★★ **Phil Lynott statue.** Pay tribute to the Boy back in town: Thin Lizzy frontman Phil Lynott stands with his bass off Grafton Street, a bronze life-size sculpture unveiled in 2005, 20 years after the singer-songwriter died aged only 36. He lived in Dublin from childhood, and

Harry Clarke's window in Bewley's.

was known for hits like *The Boys are Back in Town*, *Dancin' in the Moonlight*, and (probably my all-time favorite cover) *Whiskey in the Jar*. Talented, good-looking, and dying young, the Ace with the Bass will always be a local hero. *Harry St., outside Bruxelles.*

8 St. Anne's Church.

Looking down Anne Street off Grafton Street is your best view of the church, with its bright red door-

Pavarotti's handprints outside the Gaiety.

way and ornate Romanesque facade. Celebrating its 300th anniversary in 2007, it boasted regulars such as Bram Stoker (who married here), Wolfe Tone, and art collector Sir Hugh Lane, plus Queen Anne. Walk around the interior to gaze at its stained glass windows; Derek the eccentrically dressed verger may unlock the balcony doors to let you upstairs. Look out for the organ, built by Thomas Telford in 1834, originally water-powered and renovated in 2005, and the bread shelf, honoring Lord Newton's bequest in 1723 to leave two loaves of bread for the city's poor. And yes, this is still honored. Lunchtime concerts are held most weeks ⏱ *30 min.18 Dawson St.* ☎ *01-676 7727. www.stannschurch. ie. Free admission. Mon–Fri 10am–4pm.*

---

9 ★★ kids **Gotham Café.** Stop by for fantastic pizzas with unusual toppings at this fun cafe-restaurant, with a tiny outdoor heated terrace. The funky interior has Rolling Stone magazine covers adorning its walls, and there's great value and service. *8 South Anne St.* ☎ *01-679 5266. $.*

10 Gaiety Theatre.

Detour onto South King Street to Dublin's longest established theater in continuous production. Its curtain first went up in 1871 with Oliver Goldsmith's double bill of *She Stoops to Conquer*, followed by the burlesque *La Belle Sauvage*. Built like a traditional opera house, with Venetian facade, the baroque adornments of the dress-circle bars were created by Frank Matcham, a great theater designer of the time. Many famous dramatic and musical stars have trodden its boards over the decades, including Pavlova, Pavarotti, Sara Bernhardt, Jack Benny, and Peter O'Toole. Bronze handprints of many of these famous folk are on the ground in front of the entrance. After huge renovations in 2007, now with a larger orchestra pit and rebuilt stage, the Gaiety hosts musicals, operas, ballets, and plays. *See p 133.*

St. Anne's Church, hearing prayers for over 300 years.

Grand Canal **to Portobello**

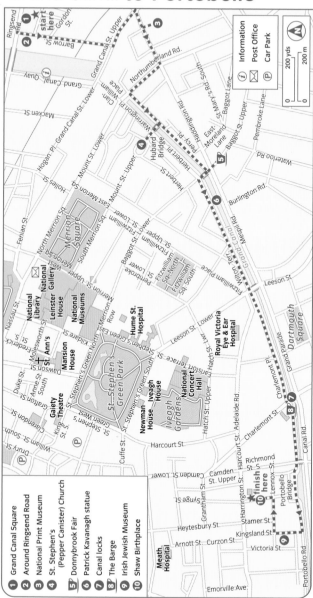

- **1** Grand Canal Square
- **2** Around Ringsend Road
- **3** National Print Museum
- **4** St. Stephen's (Pepper Canister) Church
- **5** Donnybrook Fair
- **6** Patrick Kavanagh statue
- **7** Canal locks
- **8** The Barge
- **9** Irish Jewish Museum
- **10** Shaw Birthplace

This tour starts at Grand Canal Square, twinned with the U.K.'s huge Grand Union Canal and follows the canal west, with a couple of detours. It ends in red-brick, terraced Portobello, once a working-class area and home to most of the city's Jewish community—including Leopold Bloom, the fictional Jewish hero in Joyce's *Ulysses*. START: **Bus 2, 3 & 77. DART: Grand Canal Dock.**

❶ ★ Grand Canal Square.

Enjoy the expanse of the paved concourse, hub of the recreated Docklands area, and Ocean Bar (www.oceanbar.ie), on the first floor of Millennium Tower in Charlotte Quay (pop in for an early lunch if time permits). If you continue around the back of the bar to the apartment block, you'll see an amusing and unusual exhibit: a huge concrete model of a letter, written by William Jessop, designer of the docks that opened in 1776, to the Board of the Grand Canal Co. In it, he complains about a wall that was 'shoving out at the foot and spoiling from the backing', which Jessop felt was 'in consequence of the piles not having been driven with a sufficient batter.' His ire is audible, even after all these years. See p 51, ❶.

The peaceful Grand Canal docks.

❷ ★ Around Ringsend Road.

As you emerge onto Ringsend Road, to the right you'll see the seven-floor, stone **Trinity Technology and Enterprise Campus**, a restored sugar refinery dating back to 1862 and now housing artisans' studios (visitors welcome). Opposite is what remains of **Bolands Flour Mills** (now derelict) where Eamon de Valera was in charge of the troops during the 1916 Easter Rising. This was one of several strategic points in the city the rebels used as bases; the mills covered the docks, where any troops sent to Dublin would disembark. Nearby Barrow and South Dock Streets have swathes of construction and glass apartment blocks, but you can still glimpse the original terraces down Gordon Street, towards the old gas station.

❸ ★ National Print Museum.

Located in the former Garrison Chapel of Beggar's Bush Barracks, built in the 1860s, this museum now houses a fascinating collection of artifacts and machinery from Ireland's printing industry. Laid out to resemble a 1940s print shop, today's high-tech industry is difficult to imagine when perusing the laborious art of manual typesetting and bookbinding. On the walls are framed newspaper pages from bygone decades, and the staff will no doubt direct you to one of the very few remaining original copies of the 1916 **Proclamation of Independence**, as read out by Pádraic

Pearse. The barracks are now a cozy residential square, its railings made from original cannons to remind you of the compound's former life. In the museum is the lovely Gutenberg Café with terrace. ⏱ *40 min. Garrison Chapel, Beggar's Bush, Haddington Rd.* ☎ *01-660 3770.* www.nationalprintmuseum.ie. *Admission €3.50 adults; €2 concs, €7 family. Mon–Fri 9am–5pm; Sat & Sun 2–5pm; closed Bank Hol weekends. DART: Grand Canal Dock.*

④ ★ St. Stephen's (Pepper Canister) Church.

Walk over the quaint **Huband Bridge,** built in 1791 and the canal's most ornate bridge. Take a detour and turn right up to St. Stephen's Church, nicknamed the Pepper-canister because of the shape of its dome. An Anglican church, this was the last of a series of Georgian churches established by the Church of Ireland and built in the suburbs as the population expanded. The church stands on Mount Street Crescent, the name of which is thought to derive from the mound that once stood at the corner of Fitzwilliam and Baggot Streets, where gallows were used for executions. Try and make it to one of the church's occasional concerts as the opening hours are, sadly, infrequent. Look out for Derek Fitzsimon's charming sculptures of children around the square, including outside Pepper Canister flats. ⏱ *15 min. Mount St. Cres.* ☎ *01-275 1720.* www.pepper canister.ie. *Jul & Aug: Mon–Fri 12:30–2pm. Services Sun 11am.*

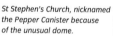

St Stephen's Church, nicknamed the Pepper Canister because of the unusual dome.

⑤ kids Donnybrook Fair.

Nip down busy Baggot Street to one of its many cafes. Better still, buy Irish cheeses, fresh salads, and breads from Donnybrook Fair deli—and check out the stunning Victorian hospital opposite. Benches dot the canal for your makeshift picnic, including one with a permanent resident (see below). *13 Baggot St.* ☎ *01-668 3556. $.*

⑥ ★★ Patrick Kavanagh statue.

Located on the north bank, opposite the floating restaurant La Peniche (p 107) sits a charming life-size sculpture of poet Patrick Kavanagh (1905–67) on a bench, acknowledging his wish, 'Oh commemorate me where there is water'. Like his drinking buddy Brendan Behan, whose statue sits along Royal Canal (see p 49, ⑧), they are remembered in these tranquil locations rather than their favorite bar McDaid's.

⑦ ★★ Canal locks.

Walking along the canal's north bank you may be lucky enough to see a boat coming through the locks, all seven of which are operated manually by lock-keepers. The last commercial barge chugged through here in 1950, but with ongoing renovation by the Inland Waterways Association of Ireland there has been an increase in canal transport, mainly for leisure. Once you reach **Portobello Bridge** (also called Le Touche), peer south down Rathmines Road to the immense pale green dome of the Church of Mary Immaculate Refuge of Sinners. Lush weeping willow trees dip into the canal's waters, where you'll also see Portobello College. On the right, red-brick terraces line the quaint narrow streets.

8 ★ **The Barge.** A canalside favorite, weekdays are quieter than raucous DJ nights. Carvery lunch is served every day, or just pick a soup and sandwich and take a seat by the water. *42 Charlemont St.* ☎ *01-475 1869. $.*

9 ★★ **Irish Jewish Museum.** Little remains of the once-thriving Jewish community here in Portobello. But this small museum housed in the old Walworth Road Synagogue has a slightly ramshackle collection of artifacts and memorabilia connected to Irish Jewry over the last 150 years, from Dublin, Belfast, Cork, and Limerick. The entrance area shows photographs (including one of my great-great-uncle's butcher shop), old paintings, certificates, and ceremonial objects. Joyce fans should look for the photos of Jewish characters as mentioned in *Ulysses.* The upper floor is the original synagogue, with religious objects displayed. The museum's volunteers can assist with genealogical research for visitors with Jewish roots in Ireland, but they do require all information in writing in advance of your visit. ⏱ *45 min.*

The Jewish Museum.

The kitchen at George Bernard Shaw's Birthplace.

3 Walworth Rd. ☎ *085-706 7357. www.jewishireland.org/museum. html. Free admission; donations welcome. May–Sept Sun, Tues & Thurs 11am–3:30pm; Oct–Apr Sun 10:30am–2:30pm.*

10 ★★★ **Shaw Birthplace.** Synge Street is the childhood home of the great playwright George Bernard Shaw (1856–1950), author of *Pygmalion, Arms and the Man,* and *Man and Superman.* My favorite parts aren't only the decent recreation of a 19th-century family home, but the revelations into Shaw's life and career, including his Nobel Prize in 1925 and an Oscar in 1938. His biting wit, as told via the audio guide, reveals his opinions of his family: his drunken father George, and mother Lucinda who 'could be classed only as a bohemian anarchist with ladylike habits' (who was also suspected of having an affair with her piano teacher). Take time afterwards to inspect everything on the walls, including a photo of Shaw signing the Freedom of the City aged 94, and with Michael Collins in 1922, shortly before Collins died. *33 Synge St.* ☎ *01-475 0854. Admission €6 adults; €5 concs; €4 children aged 3–11. Jun–Aug Tues–Fri 10am–5pm (closed 1–2pm), Sat 2–5pm.*

The Best Neighborhood Walks

Kilmainham to **Phoenix Park**

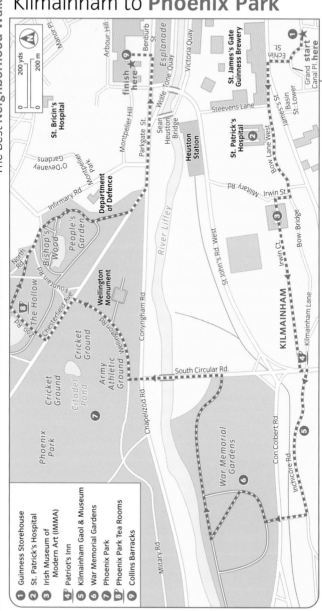

1. Guinness Storehouse
2. St. Patrick's Hospital
3. Irish Museum of Modern Art (IMMA)
4. Patriot's Inn
5. Kilmainham Gaol & Museum
6. War Memorial Gardens
7. Phoenix Park
8. Phoenix Park Tea Rooms
9. Collins Barracks

start here

finish here

St. James's Gate Guinness Brewery

St. Patrick's Hospital

St. Bricin's Hospital

Department of Defence

Wellington Monument

Heuston Station

Phoenix Park Tea Rooms

People's Garden

Bishop's Wood

The Hollow

Cricket Ground

Cricket Ground

Army Athletic Ground

Citadel Pond

Phoenix Park

War Memorial Gardens

River Liffey

KILMAINHAM

Sean Heuston Bridge

Bow Bridge

A prison, park, hospital, and barracks—plus areas rarely visited. Starting at the land of Guinness, this takes you through Kilmainham where Vikings settled 2,000 years ago, and home to the historic Gaol. After a peaceful walk to bucolic Phoenix Park, take in Collins Barracks's exhibitions if you have the energy. START: **Bus 51B, 78A and 123 to James's Street.**

❶ ★★ Guinness Storehouse.
Even if you've already explored the Storehouse, this historic area is firmly ingrained with the Guinness family. Arthur Guinness grew up at nearby 1 Thomas Street, then established the St. James's Gate Brewery in 1759, taking over a small redundant brewery (paying only a little more than the cost of a pint today). He married Olivia Whitmore, a relative of Henry Grattan, in 1761 and they had 21 children—really proving the advertizing slogan 'Guinness is good for you'. If you walk up Crane St., dating back to 1728, look down cobbled Rainsford Street (around 1700) to spot the original tram lines. The brewery was later inherited by his great-grandson Arthur, later known as the first Lord Ardilaun, and Edward, the first Earl of Iveagh; his statue stands in the grounds of St. Patrick's Cathedral, for which he paid for refurbishment. Their first family home is next door to the main gate. From here, cross the

Crane Street near the Guinness Store house dates back to 1728.

main road and veer right at the obelisk fountain topped by a sundial.

❷ ★ St. Patrick's Hospital.
Walking down Bow Lane West, you can peek into the grounds of the hospital, financed by Jonathan Swift and opened in 1757. Then the Dean

The courtyard of the Museum of Modern Art.

Harrowing history in Kilmainham Gaol.

of St. Patrick's Cathedral and governor of the city workhouse, the man better known for penning children's classic *Gulliver's Travels* was at the forefront in treating the mentally ill. This was seen to be the most enlightened institution in the British Isles, for the first time treating them as patients rather than criminals. Still operating as a psychiatric hospital, you can see the facade of his original building, designed by architect George Semple, from the southeast corner, although it doubled in size in 1778 with Thomas Cooley's additions. *James's Street.*

3 ★★★ kids **Irish Museum of Modern Art (IMMA).** Walk up Irwin Street and through the grounds of **Royal Hospital Kilmainham**, as many locals refer to it still, now home to a superb collection of modern art. Built on the site of the former priory of the Knights Hospitallers, suppressed by King Henry VIII around 1541, the foundation stones were laid in 1680 by the Viceroy, James Butler. This is the world's second oldest military hospital after Les Invalides in Paris, on which this was modeled by designer Sir William Robinson. It was a home for 300 wounded soldiers until 1928 when the remaining residents were transferred to Chelsea's Royal Hospital in

London. Opened as a museum in 1991, it has a superb permanent collection of around 6,000 works from Irish and international artists, with regularly changing temporary exhibitions and always something from its own collection. Many of the original features have been maintained and it's possible to take a tour of the Baroque Chapel (June to September), and the Heritage Room with a display of the site's history. The vast courtyard is a huge graceful space which may be dotted with sculptures, depending on current exhibitions. There are also children's activities most Sundays and through the summer. The itsa@imma cafe has a salad bar and hot dishes. Exit the grounds west through Francis Johnston's Richmond Tower, formerly a gateway to the Guinness Brewery. On the way, look out for the gravestones behind the fence including **Bully's Acre**, where pensioners from the military hospital are buried. ⏱ *1½ hr. Military Rd, Kilmainham.* ☎ *01-612 9900. www.imma.ie. Free admission. Tues–Sat 10am–5pm; Sun & Bank Hols noon–5:30pm.*

4 ★ **Patriot's Inn.** Take a break at the bar which has been the site of a tavern since 1793. Its name honors the patriots who were incarcerated or killed at the nearby gaol. These days it's a traditional pub with a decent selection of food. *760 South Circular Rd, Kilmainham* ☎ *01-679 9595. $.*

5 ★★★ kids **Kilmainham Gaol & Museum.** The decent exhibition is a good starting point, with plenty to consider regarding capital punishment. The guided tour then takes you around one of Europe's largest unoccupied jails—a harrowing history lesson. This was the site of numerous executions of political prisoners including most leaders of the 1916 Easter Rising, and events occurring here have shaped the country's history. Kilmainham had rejected the old-style gaol where many shared a cell, and instead had individual cells for each person where everyone had to be silent, based on London's Pentonville Prison. But it was soon overcrowded, especially during the Famine years

Huge Wellington Monument in Phoenix Park.

Children's bikes for hire at Phoenix Park.

from 1845, when prisoners were the destitute caught stealing food. Highlights—and the grimmest bits—of the tour are the individual cells that housed so many famous names at the heart of the struggle for independence, including Robert Emmet, Charles Stuart Parnell, and Eamon de Valera. The tour ends at the exercise yard, where the lives of so many ended by hanging or the firing squad: these include 1916 Easter Rising leaders James Connolly, Joseph Plunkett (who had married in the prison's chapel ten minutes earlier), Thomas Clarke, and Pádraic Pearse. In recent years, more than 70 films have been shot here including *Michael Collins, The Italian Job,* and an opera. Suitable for older children. ⏱ *1½ hr. Inchicore Rd, Kilmainham.* ☎ *01-453 5984. Admission €6 adults, €4 seniors, €2 children 10–15 yrs/students, €14 family. Apr–Sept: Daily 9:30am–6pm; Oct–Mar Mon–Sat 9:30am–5:30pm; Sun 10am–6pm. Last admission 1 hr before close.*

6 ★★ kids **War Memorial Gardens.** Turn right onto Memorial Road and cross the busy Con Colbert Road to enter the peaceful gardens designed by Sir Edwin Lutyens and opened in 1939. The memorial commemorates more than 49,000

Collins Barracks.

Irishmen killed in action during World War I, their names recorded in the granite bookrooms. The gardens are a delight to wander around, with surprisingly few people visiting the fragrant rose garden, fountains, and lily ponds. Walk towards the north and when you hit the Liffey, turn right and keep walking—you'll pass the **University Boat House** and then **hurling grounds**. (There is a lovely walk if you turn left at the river, although lone visitors may find it too deserted.) At the exit gates, take the right-hand fork, then turn left onto South Circular Road.

7 ★★★ **kids Phoenix Park.** You may have already explored the huge park—one of the world's largest—with its myriad attractions. You'll enter the park near the huge

Wellington Monument obelisk, so either cut through and exit via Park Gate, take time to explore and spot deer, or hire a bicycle (see p 29). If you don't have the time or energy, pop into the nearby **People's Garden** with its Victorian layout (p 96, **10**). ⏱ *1 hr. See Chapter 5, section Phoenix Park.*

8 ★ **Phoenix Park Tea Rooms.** A simple little cafe, not much more than a wooden hut, but with great coffee, paninis, and cakes, and tables outside so you really feel out in the open. Or you could take your refreshments and sprawl out on some suitable grassy area. *Opp entrance to Dublin Zoo, Phoenix Park.* ☎ *01-671 4431. $.*

9 ★★ **kids Collins Barracks.** Home to the highly recommended **National Museum of Decorative Arts and History**, this imposing structure was originally the Royal Barracks and was renamed in 1922. The initial buildings, designed by architect Captain Thomas Burgh and completed in 1706, with additional buildings later, went on to house troops for nearly 300 years. Built around a series of open squares—of which the main courtyard is perfect for getting a sense of its scale—it once housed up to 5,000 soldiers and the signs still remain on its walls for marching practice. Europe's oldest inhabited barracks, it was decommissioned in 1996 after which it was taken over by the National Museum. ⏱ *1½ hr. See p 57, **8**.* ●

Shopping Best Bets

Best **Bargain-hunting for Fashionistas**
★★ Penney's, *35–39 Lower O'Connell St.* (p 81)

Best **Streetwear for Well-heeled Teens**
★ BT2, *28–29 Grafton St.* (p 78)

Best for **Haggling over Tomatoes**
★ Moore Street Market, *Moore St.* (p 84)

Best for **Designer Baby Clothes**
★★ Milk + Cookies, *14 Westbury Mall, Clarendon St.* (p 83)

Best for **Handmade Engagement Rings**
★★ Design Yard, *48–49 Nassau St.* (p 86)

Best for **Full-On Foodies**
★★★ Fallon & Byrne, *11–17 Exchequer St.* (p 81)

Best for **Kitting Out for Winter**
★★ Trinity Sweaters, *30 Nassau St.* (p 81)

Best for **Vintage Earrings**
★★ Rhinestones, *18 St. Andrews St.* (p 86)

Best for **Traditional Irish Penny Whistles**
★ Charles Byrne Musik Instrumente, *21–22 Lower Stephen St.* (p 85)

Best **Classy Department Store**
★★★ Brown Thomas, *88–95 Grafton St.* (p 78)

Best for **Quirky New Art**
★★ Bad Art Gallery, *79 Francis St.* (p 76)

Best for **Pink Handbags**
★ Costelloe + Costelloe, *14A Chatham St.* (p 85)

High street stores on South King Street.

Best for **Art Books**
★★ Noble & Beggarman, *28 South William St.* (p 77)

Best for **Trad Irish Music Musing**
★★ Celtic Note, *14–15 Nassau St.* (p 85)

Best for **Gents' Handmade Suits**
★★ Louis Copeland, *18–19 Wicklow St.* (p 80)

Best for **Eclectic Market Browsing**
★★ George's St Arcade, *South Great George's St.* (p 84)

Best for **Contemporary Irish Art**
★★ Kevin Sharkey Gallery, *80 Francis St.* (p 76)

Best for a **Claddagh Ring**
★★ College House Jewelers, *44 Nassau St.* (p 85)

Best for **Last-minute Souvenirs**
★ Tourism Centre, *Suffolk St.* (p 83)

Best for **Gorgeous Chocolates**
★ Butlers Chocolate Café, *51A Grafton St.* (p 81)

Previous page: Cheese galore at Temple Bar food market.

Grafton & Nassau Streets

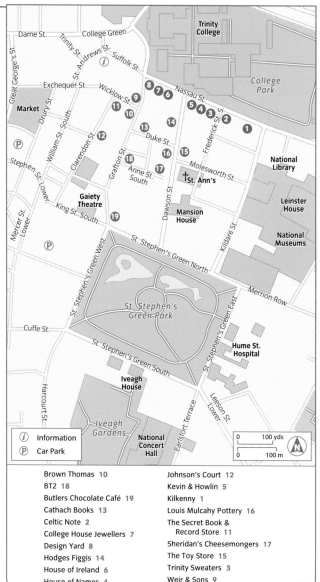

Dublin Shopping

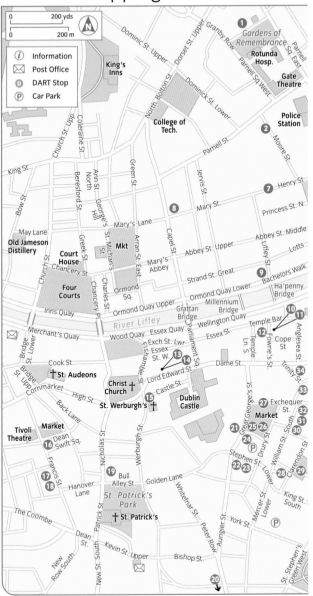

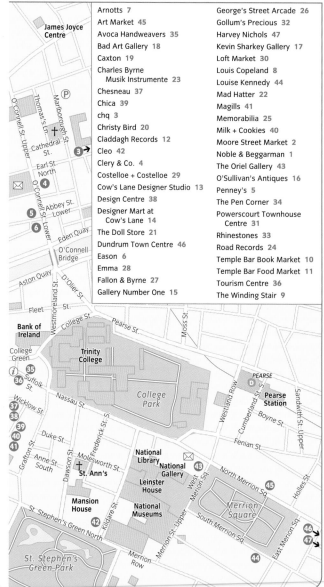

Dublin **Shopping A to Z**

Antiques & Art

★★ Bad Art Gallery Vibrant art at affordable prices, this is a bright, spacious gallery, perfect for browsing large-scale artwork. More than 30 of today's best Irish artists have work here, with at least 200 pieces on display. Great fun and friendly staff. *79 Francis St.* ☎ *01-453 7588. www.thebadartgallerydublin.com. AE, MC, V. Map p 74.*

★ Caxton An eye-popping amount of antique prints suitable for serious collectors packed into a tiny space: etchings, prints, engravings, and miniature landscapes dating between 1500 and the 1800s, from all over the world. *63 Patrick St.* ☎ *01-453 0060. No credit cards. Map p 74.*

★ Christy Bird Antique furniture has been sold at this family-owned store since 1945. With quirky collectables, you might unearth a Tiffany lamp, an old brass phone, or stained-glass fire screen. *32 South Richmond St.* ☎ *01-475 4049. www. christybird.com. MC, V. Map p 74.*

★ Gallery Number One This cheerful gallery which opened in 2007 is home to archived photos of rock stars plus regularly changing exhibitions specializing in pop art and pop music. It features up-and-coming local artists and photographers. *1 Castle St.* ☎ *01-478 9090. www.gallerynumberone.com. AE, MC, V. Map p 74.*

★★ Kevin Sharkey Gallery Celebrity Irish artist Sharkey brings a touch of glam to Dublin's art scene with large-scale stunning abstract paintings on show. His high profile brings a high price tag to match. *80 Francis St.* ☎ *(mobile) 086-376 0622. www.kevinsharkey. com. AE, MC, V. Map p 74.*

★ The Oriel Gallery Ireland's oldest independent gallery, founded in 1968, still sets out to promote and exhibit quality Irish paintings and mounts group exhibitions. It's renowned for its collection of the late Markey Robinson, a troubled Belfast artist who outsells everyone else. *17 Clare St.* ☎ *01-676 3410. www.the oriel.com. MC, V. Map p 74.*

★★ O'Sullivan's Antiques One of several decent antiques stores on the street, this specializes in Georgian and early Victorian furniture (with a branch in New York). Filled with elegant chairs, chandeliers, and watercolors, this is for the serious collector. *43–44 Francis St.* ☎ *01-454 1143. www.osullivan antiques.com. AE, MC, V. Map p 74.*

Books & Stationery

★ Cathach Books Member of the Antiquarian Booksellers Association, this isn't the store for a bestselling thriller. With second-hand rare

Cathach Books for serious bibliophiles.

The relaxing Winding Stair.

books, signed copies, and first editions, and the hushed tone of a library, this is for serious bibliophiles. *10 Duke St.* ☎ *01-671 8676. www.rarebooks.ie. AE, MC, V. Map p 73.*

★ **Eason**   Going strong since 1819, Eason's flagship store has a staggering selection over its four floors. Browse Irish and international fiction, history, photography, and biographies, then sink into its cafe to recover. (Smaller branches citywide.) *40 Lower O'Connell St.* ☎ *01-858-3800. www.eason.ie. AE, MC, V. Map p 74.*

★★ **Hodges Figgis**   Close to Trinity College, this is a favorite with academics and houses a mammoth collection of pretty much everything. Wonderful for browsing, it has a fantastic bargain basement (literally) with cut-price books. *56–58 Dawson St.* ☎ *01-677 4754. AE, MC, V. Map p 73.*

★★ **Noble & Beggarman**   This small independent bookstore is packed full of books on Irish art, photography, architecture, design, and art theory, in a new venue. (Also at Royal Hibernian Academy.) *28 South William St.* ☎ *01-633 3568. www.nobleandbeggarmanbooks.com. MC, V. Map p 74.*

★ **The Pen Corner**   For lovers of fountain pens, this stationery store has been selling stylish writing gear since 1927. Its basement has a lovely collection of unusual and arty cards and notepaper, the antithesis to the computer keyboard. *12 College Green.* ☎ *01-679 3641. AE, MC, V. Map p 74.*

★ **The Secret Book & Record Store**   Tucked away down an alley off Wicklow St., this is crammed with hundreds of new and second-hand books. The owner only buys what he likes, so there's little dross here; great for a holiday read or a heavyweight tome. *15A Wicklow St.* ☎ *01-679 7272. MC, V. Map p 73.*

★ **The Winding Stair**   A famous literary landmark since the 1970s, new management has retained the original style. More second-hand, new books, and unusual titles than popular bestsellers, with fantastic leather sofas to make browsing a pleasure. *40 Ormond Quay.* ☎ *01-872 6576. www.winding-stair.com. MC, V. Map p 74.*

Department Stores

★ **Arnotts**   Ireland's oldest department store (est. 1843) is also the largest. The Dublin section in Sportswear has all replica Gaelic

National institution Clery's.

games team kits. Safe without being over-savvy, labels include Mango, Boss, Diesel, plus household and beauty. *12 Henry St.* ☎ *01-805 0400. www.arnotts.ie. AE, MC, V. Map p 74.*

★★★ **Brown Thomas** The top-hatted doorman sets the scene, although there's nothing snooty about its service. Great for men's and women's fashions and household gifts, shop for Ralph Lauren, Marc Jacobs, Karen Millen, and Gucci, before a manicure at Nails Inc or facial at Jo Malone. *88–95 Grafton St.* ☎ *01-605 6666. www.brown thomas.com. AE, MC, V. Map p 73.*

★★ **Clery & Co.** Located in a listed building on busy O'Connell Street, Clery's (est. 1853) enjoyed a huge revamp in 2004 but retains original architectural touches. Karen Millen, Mexx, Topshop, East, Ben Sherman, Levi, and Van Heusen cater for men and women of all ages, and there's a wonderful homeware department. *18–27 Lower O'Connell St.* ☎ *01-878-6000. www.clerys.com. AE, DC, MC, V. Map p 74.*

★ **Harvey Nichols** With a sumptuous foodmarket and restaurant popular with 'ladies who lunch', this

glam store is the main draw in the new Dundrum Mall, south of the center. Very hip and label-conscious, it features all the top designers and also has a large accessories department. *Dundrum Town Center, Sandyford Rd.* ☎ *01-291 0488. www. harveynichols.com. AE, DC, MC, V. LUAS: Balally. Map p 74.*

Fashion & Clothing

★ kids **BT2** An offshoot of Brown Thomas department store (left), this has top contemporary fashion labels for men and women's urban wear, including Miss Sixty, All Saints, G-Star, and Juicy Couture, plus funky tees from Goi Goi. *28–29 Grafton St.* ☎ *01-605 6666. www.bt2.ie. AE, MC, V. Map p 73.*

★★ **Chica** This is the place to come for beaded tops, dressy fabrics, and eccentric outfits to make a real statement. Or just try the chunky bangles and rings the size of dinner plates, keeping on the right side of good taste. *Unit 25, Westbury*

Glittery goodies at Chica.

Tweed trilbies at Kevin & Howlin.

Mall, Harry St. ☎ 01-633 4441. *www.chicaboutiqueonline.com.* MC, V. Map p 74.

★★ **Cleo**   A family business since 1936 specializing in hand-knitted sweaters, Cleo loves natural fabrics and Irish handmade clothing made by artisans from all over Ireland. Fabulous unique styles include felt coats, capes, and alpaca sweaters— some with 700-year-old 'bog yew' buttons. *18 Kildare St.* ☎ *01-676 1421. www.cleo-ltd.com. AE, MC, V. Map p 74.*

Cow's Lane Designer Studio So much is crammed into this one store, a collaboration of Dublin-based designers and artists, many with stalls at Designer Mart at Cow's Lane (see p 84). All clothing, accessories, and furnishings are handmade, and you might be able to meet the designer in person. *West Essex St. No phone. No credit cards. Map p 74.*

★ **Design Centre**   The top floor of the Powerscourt Centre has contemporary styles from Irish designers including John Rocha, Philip Treacy, and Pauric Sweeney, plus Kenzo and Jasmine De Milo. Fashionistas will love it. *Powerscourt*

Centre, South William St. ☎ *01-679 5718. www.designcentre.ie. AE, MC, V. Map p 74.*

★ **Emma**   This gorgeous boutique sells flowing, feminine designs including Susie Wong and Pink Soda Urban, along with flower-enhanced or beaded accessories, so you know that you'll get a unique outfit. *33 Clarendon St.* ☎ *01-633 9781. www. emma.ie. MC, V. Map p 75.*

★ **Kevin & Howlin**   Get kitted out in top pepper-and-salt or herringbone Irish tweeds, especially hand-woven Donegal. The store has a fine range of men's wool suits, coats, traditional tweed hats and scarves, plus smart ladies' suits. The store can make to order and ship. *31 Nassau St.* ☎ *01-677 0257. www.kevinandhowlin.com. AE, MC, V. Map p 73.*

★★ **Loft Market**   Not exactly a market, more like a collection of young local designers on the top floor of the Powerscourt Centre, who are often there in person. One-off designs include revamped vintage gear, hand-beaded silks and embroidered raw silks, plus chunky clay jewelry. *Powerscourt Centre,*

South William St. ☎ 01-671 7000.
No credit cards. Map p 74.

★★ **Louis Copeland**   The Cope-
lands have been famed throughout
Ireland for generations for their top-
quality suits. The store carries
labels like Hugo Boss, Canali, and
snazzy Duchamp ties, and they'll
make free alterations. (Four other
outlets.) 39–41 Capel St. ☎ 01-872
1600. www.louiscopeland.com. AE,
MC, V. Map p 74.

★★ **Louise Kennedy**   Oozing
style, located in a Georgian house,
award-winning Kennedy's top fashions sit easily with her own designs
in Tipperary Crystal, plus David Lin-
ley furniture and Philip Treacy hats.
Top-class products with price tags
to match seduce a select clientele.
56 Merrion Square. ☎ 01-662 0056.
www.louisekennedy.com. AE, MC, V.
Map p 74.

Prime Shopping Zones

Centerpiece to the Southside's shopping experience is the
pedestrianized **Grafton Street** with Brown Thomas, Weir, and a
host of reliable fashion chains, all heaving at weekends. Running off
that is **Johnson's Court** alleyway with diamond jewelry aplenty,
leading to the majestic **Powerscourt Townhouse Centre,** which
contains an antiques arcade and the Design Centre. Near Trinity
College, **Nassau Street** has a good collection of shops for quality
crafts and gifts, including Kilkenny and House of Ireland, and **Dawson Street** has bookstores. For antique furniture and jewelry head
to **Francis Street** near St. Patrick's Cathedral. In the southern suburbs, the huge **Dundrum
Town Centre** attempts to
lure shoppers away from the
center, with a vast mall of
upmarket high-street names
including Harvey Nichols.
Temple Bar has weekend
outdoor markets, quirky
clothes, and record stores.
North of the Liffey, vast
O'Connell Street houses the
much-loved department store
Clery's, plus Eason bookstore
and Penney's for cheap fashions. Near that is **Henry
Street,** once a big shopping
area but less popular these
days, with department store
Arnotts, and **Moore Street**
market running off that.

View from Bewley's onto Grafton Street.

Fallon & Byrne for foodies.

★★ **kids** **Penney's** Get ready to rummage: owned by Primark in the U.K., this is the place for cheery fashions and accessories for adults and kids at fantastic value. The clothes might not last for years, but at that price, who cares? Hugely popular and always packed, try to avoid the scrum on a Saturday. *35–39 Lower O'Connell St. ☎ 01-666 6656. www. primark.ie. MC, V. Map p 74.*

★★ **kids** **Trinity Sweaters** Specializing in Irish knitwear and giftware, you can find all types of woollies from contemporary knits to heavy Aran or merino wool sweaters. Look out for the designer clearance upstairs. *30 Nassau St. ☎ 01-671 2292. www. sweatershop.ie. MC, V. Map p 73.*

Gourmet Food
★ **Butlers Chocolate Café** Still using the original 1932 recipes from Ms Bailey-Butler, the small stores dotted around town sell their gorgeous chocs by the box or individually, including orange marzipan, *cerise au kirsch*, and Irish cream liqueur. Its cafe also sells freshly brewed coffee and, of course, hot chocolate. *51A Grafton St. ☎ 01-616 7004. www.butlers chocolates.com. AE, MC, V. Map p 73.*

★★★ **Fallon & Byrne** The mother of all food halls (and one where I'd happily spend a year) sells everything from designer truffles and fresh fruit tarts to charcuterie and organic vegetables. This has the selection of a supermarket but the class of a boutique. *11–17 Exchequer St. ☎ 01-472 1010. www.fallonand byrne.com. MC, V. Map p 74.*

★ **Magills** A cozy little deli established in the 1920s so it still has that old-fashioned feel, which is no bad thing. It has an excellent charcuterie counter, plus cheeses, jars of herbs, Italian panforte, and homemade chutneys. *14 Clarendon St. ☎ 01-671 3830. MC, V. Map p 74.*

★★★ **Sheridan's Cheesemongers** The place to stock up for a top-class picnic, Sheridan's offers nearly 100 cheeses from around the world, including handmade Irish cheeses such as Wicklow Blue Brie and Knockanore Smoked. The store also sells a few select top-quality items like Ortiz tuna, Aran smoked salmon, olives, and breads. Try the takeaway sandwiches at lunchtimes. *11 South Anne St. ☎ 01-679 3143. www.sheridanscheesemongers.com. MC, V. Map p 73.*

Household & Gifts

★★ kids Avoca Handweavers

A feast of decorative homeware, like flowery tea canisters and embroidered cushions, plus retro chic fashions and a gourmet food hall. Beautifully laid out, the jewelry, ceramics, and Avoca Anthology designer womenswear are hard to resist. Kids' clothes and toys are on the upper floors. *11–13 Suffolk St.* ☎ *01-677 4215. www.avoca.ie. MC, V. Map p 74.*

★ House of Ireland

Pick your way carefully between the displays of creamy Belleek ceramics, John Rocha-designed Waterford crystal, Claddagh rings, and Mullingar Pewter goblets in a showcase of traditional homeware. *38 Nassau St.* ☎ *01-671 1111. www.houseofireland. com. AE, DC, MC, V. Map p 73.*

★ House of Names

For anyone with Irish roots, House of Names is a great place to visit for heraldic souvenirs, ranging from keyrings to robust copper shields. Framed certificates with family name, origin, and meaning take 10 days, and can be ordered in advance by phone or e-mail. *26 Nassau St.* ☎ *01-679 7287. www.houseofnames.ie. AE, MC, V. Map p 73. Also at 8 Fleet St.* ☎ *01-677 7034.*

★★ Kilkenny

Drop by Dublin's best emporium for Irish-made gifts and arty finds for home, with Waterford crystal, ceramics, and contemporary sculptures. Don't miss the Irish fashions with local designers like Aideen Bodkin and Quin & Donnelly. There's a decent restaurant upstairs (see p 8). *5–6 Nassau St.* ☎ *01-677 7066. www.kilkennyshop. com. AE, DC, MC, V. Map p 73.*

★★ Louis Mulcahy Pottery

Individually designed pieces of attractive stoneware from this workshop, going strong for 40 years. His work is known for its strength and durability, and includes colorful tableware and hand-thrown lamp bases. *46 Dawson St.* ☎ *01-670 9311. www.louismulcahy.com. MC, V. Map p 73.*

★ Memorabilia

This quirky market stall sells retro posters, those

Sumptuous household goods at Avoca.

Weekend Art Market at Merrion Square.

famous 1940s Guinness ads plus Jameson's advertizing plates. Ideal for stocking up on small fun gifts. *Unit 7, George's St Arcade. No phone. No credit cards. Map p 74.*

★ **Tourism Centre**   Housed in the former Church of St. Andrew, the store in the tourist office is chock-full of inexpensive souvenirs, from T-shirts and posters to Irish biscuits. It makes a good last-minute shop stop before hopping on the airport bus. *Suffolk St.* ☎ *01-605 7700. www.visitdublin.com. MC, V. Map p 74.*

Kids

★ **The Doll Store**   A large range of top-quality miniatures to furnish a doll's house, traditional Teddy bears, and celeb dolls. Little ones can even 'create a doll', choosing body, hair, features, and clothes, so it'll be difficult to drag them out. *62 South Great George's St.* ☎ *01-478 3403. www.dollstore.ie. MC, V. Map p 74.*

★★ **Milk + Cookies**   A clothes store for young kids, this is designer without being flashy. Utterly charming styles; outfits here are more

like miniatures of good-taste adult clothes in top-quality fabrics, albeit with high prices. *14 Westbury Mall.* ☎ *01-671 0104. www.milkandcookies dublin.com. MC, V. Map p 74.*

★★ **The Toy Store**   Goodies range from soft toys for newborns to Scalextric and build-your-own Star Wars spaceships. A huge range packed into a relatively small space, the emphasis is on crafts, rather than anything too gadget-like. *13–17 Dawson St.* ☎ *01-677 4420. MC, V. Map p 73.*

Markets & Malls

★ **Art Market**   Springing up at weekends from around 11am and busiest on Sundays during summer, the outside of Merrion Square is filled with local amateur artists pinning up their work on the railings. Although not all of it is great quality, you might discover a gem if you're persistent. *Merrion Square. Map p 74.*

★ **chq**   Built from a famous tobacco warehouse, this sleek shopping center houses select stores including top tailor **Louis Copeland,** ladies' boutique **Fran & Jane,**

The Shopping Fine Print

Ireland is a little slow to get moving in the morning, with most stores opening at 10am. Standard shopping hours are Monday to Saturday 10am to 6pm, with no closure for lunch. Sunday shopping, once seen as a taboo in this Catholic land, is popular and seen as necessary for many stores (except for modest family-run ones) opening around 11am or noon to 4 or 5pm. Most stores also open late on Thursday evenings, until around 8pm. Sales can happen pretty much year round with the usual clearance after Christmas, although many fashion stores seem to have a huge Sale notice in their windows in the spring and summer. For information on sales tax and related rebates for non E.U. residents, see p 170.

and home accessories at **Meadows and Byrne**. *The chq Building, IFSC, Docklands. www.chq.ie. Map p 74.*

★★ **Designer Mart at Cow's Lane** Growing slowly since 2007, this Saturday market now showcases 30 artists and designers from around Ireland, including handmade jewelry, funky fashion, and furniture. *Cows Lane, Temple Bar. Map p 74.*

★ **Dundrum Town Centre** This huge mall south of the city center, easily accessible by Luas tram, specializes in popular high-street chains such as Esprit, French Connection, Mexx, and Zara, with jewelers, restaurants, kids' gear, sportswear, and stationery, plus Harvey Nichols (see p 78) as a designer highlight for many. *Sandyford Rd.* ☎ *01-299 1700. www.dundrum.ie. LUAS: Balally. Map p 74.*

★★ kids **George's St Arcade**
The former red-brick Victorian meat market is now home to quirky stalls, including vintage clothing and footwear at **Wild Child,** second-hand records at **Spin Dizzy,** and jewelry at **Barry Doyle Design**. *South Great George's St. www.georgesstreet arcade.ie. Map p 74.*

★ **Moore Street Market** Hardly the place it once was, but Moore Street is still one of the few remaining genuine daily street markets (Monday to Saturday) with stalls of cheap fruit, veg, and foodstuffs from farther afield like Asia and Africa. Stop by to watch the deliveries by horse-and-cart and listen to fruity banter. *Moore St. Map p 74.*

★★ **Powerscourt Townhouse Centre** With 18th-century history and graceful decor, the center houses the **Antique Gallery,** fashion stores, lovely independent jewelry stores, plus the **Design Centre** and **Loft Market** on the top floor. The Atrium has plenty of eating places on both floors. *59 South William St.* ☎ *01-671 7000. www.powerscourt centre.com. Map p 74.*

★ **Temple Bar Book Market**
A small but handy selection of second-hand books every weekend, mainly by Irish authors but also international best-sellers: good for a holiday paperback read. Stalls also deal in second-hand CDs and rare vinyl. *Temple Bar Square. Map p 74.*

★ Temple Bar Food Market
Every Saturday sees the main square filled with the farmers' market selling organic fruit and veg, Irish cheeses, homemade breads and cakes, and freshly cooked snacks; a relatively new concept, which seems to attract more visitors than locals. *Meeting House Square, Temple Bar. Map p 74.*

Music

★★ Celtic Note
This longstanding Dublin favorite is a great place to get to know Irish music, whether classical, folk, roots, or contemporary. It has a good range of CDs and DVDs, and is also an excellent place to find out about live music events and to buy tickets. *14–15 Nassau St.* ☎ *01-670 4157. www.celticnote. com. AE, MC, V. Map p 73.*

★ Charles Byrne Musik Instrumente
The charming old gent in charge comes from a music-loving family and hand-makes violins at this store, going strong since 1870. Specializing in stringed instruments, it's also the best place in town to choose a banjo, Irish wooden flute, penny whistle, and even a book on how to play them. *21–22 Lower*

Bags of color at Costelloe & Costelloe.

Stephen St. ☎ *01-478 1773. www. charlesbyrne.com. AE, MC, V. Map p 74.*

★ Claddagh Records
More than just a much-loved music store, it has a history as a record label specializing in Irish sounds and traditional music. A lovely, friendly place to browse. *2 Cecilia St, Temple Bar.* ☎ *01-677 0262. www.claddagh records.com. MC, V. Map p 74.*

★ Road Records
Independent music store specializing in left-field, non-chart music, especially Irish-based independent artists. The kind of place you can come across the unusual! *16b Fade St.* ☎ *01-671 7340. www.roadrecs.com. MC. V. Map p 74.*

Shoes & Accessories

★ Chesneau
Established by French-born, Kilkenny-based Edmond Chesneau, the bags are top quality, simple styles, and elegant with a good selection in all colors, ranging from petite evening bags to huge carrying devices that accommodate piles of books. *37 Wicklow St.* ☎ *01-672 9199. www.chesneau design.com. MC, V. Map p 74.*

★★ College House Jewellers
Specializing in Celtic jewelry, this is the place if you want to buy and learn about a Claddagh (Irish love or friendship) ring or pendant. Hugely popular, it gives decent discounts to overseas visitors. *44 Nassau St.* ☎ *01-677 7597. www. collegehousejewellers.com. AE, MC, V. Map p 73.*

★ Costelloe + Costelloe
A fantastic range of fun, girly handbags, wraps, and bangles in a rainbow hue of colors with an eye-catching, busy window display. Bring your new outfit here and you're guaranteed to find a match. *14A Chatham St.* ☎ *01-671 4209.*

www.costelloeandcostelloe.com. AE, MC, V. Map p 74.

★★ **Design Yard** This collective of contemporary designers, creating jewelry, sculpture, and applied arts, stocks mainly one-off pieces by Irish designers. The four-floor space includes a gallery showcasing local artists, plus an amazing collection of handmade diamond engagement rings. *48–49 Nassau St.* ☎ *01-474 1011. www.designyardgallery.com. AE, MC, V. Map p 73.*

★★ **Gollum's Precious** Designer jewelry from throughout the world, especially Paris, but they also make many of their own beaded pieces, keeping costs down. High fashion but good quality, using unusual materials such as plated glass and colorful silver designs. *Powerscourt Centre.* ☎ *01-670 5400. MC, V. Map p 74.*

★ **Johnson's Court** Not just one but a cluster of classy jewelers on this tiny alleyway. Try **Appleby** for large-scale diamond creations, **Paul Sheeran** for watches, and **Gray's** for freshwater pearls. *Johnson's Court, Grafton St. Map p 73.*

★★★ **Mad Hatter** Fantastic hats and headgear from local designer Nessa Cronin, who uses unusual fabrics such as sinamay (banana plant). The colorful collection includes eye-catching, creative hats and crystal-adorned headpieces, suitable for the mother of the bride or a day at the races. *20 Lower Stephen St.* ☎ *01-405 4936. www.madhatterhat.com. AE, MC, V. Map p 74.*

★★ **Rhinestones** Antique, vintage, and costume jewelry fill this gorgeous store, where pieces are unusual and quirky, and all high quality. Specialties include silver, 1950s painted glass, and Art Deco pieces. *18 St. Andrew St.* ☎ *01-679 0759. AE, MC, V. Map p 74.*

★★ **Weir & Sons** Longstanding Grafton Street jewelers since 1869, and a class act, Weir and Sons carry all the top names in jewelry, watches, and antique silver such as Fabergé, Rolex, and Cartier. Walk-in shoppers are welcome and service is impeccable. Look out for the original door from 1895. *96–99 Grafton St.* ☎ *01-677 9678. www.weirandsons.ie. AE, DC, MC, V. Map p 73.* ●

Fantastic headwear at Mad Hatter.

The Best of the Outdoors

St. Stephen's Green &
Iveagh Gardens

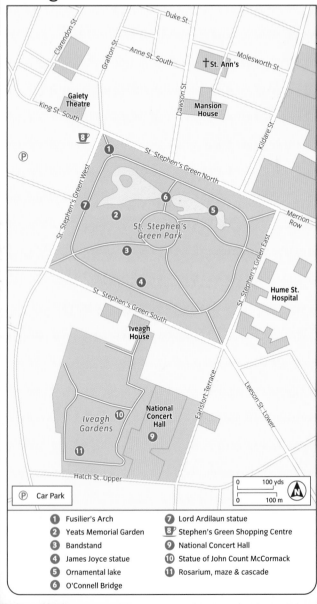

1 Fusilier's Arch	**7** Lord Ardilaun statue
2 Yeats Memorial Garden	**8** Stephen's Green Shopping Centre
3 Bandstand	**9** National Concert Hall
4 James Joyce statue	**10** Statue of John Count McCormack
5 Ornamental lake	**11** Rosarium, maze & cascade
6 O'Connell Bridge	

Ⓟ Car Park

St. Stephen's Green is adored by locals, who flock to its verdant lawns at the first sight of the sun. You can relax here for hours, explore the grounds dotted with sculptures, and enjoy the music and performances. Just a minute's walk away are the tranquil Iveagh Gardens, exquisite in their near desolation. Nearby, yet a world away. START: **Northwest corner of St. Stephen's Green.** ⏱ **2 hr.**

1 ★ **Fusiliers' Arch.** The huge Ballyknockan granite arch, nearly 10m (33 ft) high, marks the northwest entrance to St. Stephen's Green. Built in 1907, and a replica of the Arch of Titus in Rome, it's a memorial to young Irish soldiers who died in the Boer War between 1899 and 1900. Stand underneath to read the engraved names of more than 230 who fell in battle. Republicans unofficially renamed it as Traitors' Gate, as this war was seen as a fight between Imperialist and Republican ideals and far from the Irish struggle. Sharp eyes might see the bullet marks on the northeast face around the words '*Laings Nek*', thought to be from the 1916 Uprising. *NW corner of St. Stephen's Green.*

2 ★★ kids **Yeats Memorial Garden.** One of my favorites in St. Stephen's Green is the bronze sculpture by British artist Henry Moore of William Butler Yeats. Made in 1967, *Knife Edge* portrays the angular looks of the Dublin-born Nobel Prize-winning author and poet, who was a founder of the Irish Literary Revival of the late 19th century. It stands at the edge of the Yeats Memorial Garden, a small amphitheater with occasional theatrical performances in summer.

3 ★ **Bandstand.** As befitting any garden of the era, this typical piece of Victoriana has cast-iron supports and a wooden roof. Built to celebrate Queen Victoria's Jubilee in 1888, it hosts lunchtime concerts on most summer days (check the noticeboard at the northwest entrance for listings) ranging from jazz and folk to swing. Most concerts start around 1pm, so lie back and enjoy. All that's missing is a decent cafe nearby.

4 ★★★ kids **James Joyce statue.** Near the bandstand, poor

The names of fallen soldiers are written under the Fusiliers' Arch.

Contrasting Spaces

The nine hectares (22 acres) of St. Stephen's Green have been a popular public space in the city center for locals ever since 1880 when Lord Ardilaun opened them up—not bad for a former leper colony and public hanging spot. But if St. Stephen's Green is a public park, **Iveagh Gardens** is the secret garden, all statues with missing arms, fountains, wooded walks, and Gothic, ivy-clad corners. Built by Ninian Niven in 1863, this was originally the private gardens of Iveagh House. Many locals say it's the city's best-kept secret, although since hosting the **Taste of Dublin Food Festival** (www.tastefestivals.ie) every June from 2007 it may not be for much longer. Both gardens are open Monday to Saturday from 8am and on Sunday from 10am. Closing time at St. Stephen's Green is 20 minutes before darkness; Iveagh Gardens closes at 6pm (Mar–Oct); 4pm (Nov–Feb).

old James Joyce makes a meek figure, tiny head mounted on a huge plinth. Now considered to be Ireland's most celebrated writer, it's strange to think that he was rejected by his own people at the time, who considered him to be far too liberal and out of step with the prevailing middle-class, Catholic, conservative culture of the time. St. Stephen's Green was one of several prominent landmarks that epitomized 'dear, dirty Dublin' for him, although he spent most of his life in self-appointed exile. Follow his gaze over the road to Newman House (p 35, ⑫), once the Catholic University where he studied.

⑤ ★★ kids **Ornamental lake.** The artificial lake stretches across the northern end of the green, built by Arthur Guinness as part of his landscaping for public enjoyment. The lake, fed by an artificial waterfall

near the bridge, is a big hit with kids, especially if they can get to feed the ducks swimming past.

⑥ ★★ kids **O'Connell Bridge.** No, not the immense multi-lane highway crossing the Liffey but a little, stone, humpbacked bridge over the lake. It's thought to be the original O'Connell Bridge, designed by J.F. Fuller at the time of the green's redesign, and built over the middle of the lake. It wasn't until 1882 that the 'other' bridge was renamed from Carlisle to O'Connell, after the lawyer who fought for Catholic rights.

⑦ ★★ kids **Lord Ardilaun statue.** It's only fitting that the man who financed and created the green has such an imposing statue. The seated figure of Lord Ardilaun looks towards the Guinness brewery at St. James's Gate. Better

Lord Ardilaun.

known as Arthur Guinness, born in 1840 and great-grandson of the original Arthur Guinness, he was something of a philanthropist, not least for purchasing the green in 1877 and giving it to the capital as a public park. As well as financing all the work, he also secured an Act of Parliament that entrusted the maintenance to the Public Works commissioners. Dubliners have much to be grateful to the dynasty for, not just because of the brew.

8 ★ kids Stephen's Green Shopping Centre. If a picnic's not possible, the food court at the glass-atrium shopping mall has a bundle of food options. Try **O'Brien's** and **La Croissanterie** for takeout sandwiches or burgers and the juice bar at **Foodlife** on the top floor. *St. Stephen's Green West. $.*

9 ★★ National Concert Hall. My favorite way of walking between St. Stephen's Green to Iveagh Gardens is via the side of the National Concert Hall (NCH) on Earlsfort Terrace. It was originally built for the Dublin International Exhibition in 1865, lasting six months, and attracting nearly one million visitors. Redeveloped in 1914 by Rudolph Maximilian in a classical style similar to Custom House, it was taken over by University College Dublin, and has been a concert hall since 1981 and owned by the NCH since 2006. Despite impressive events, the venue is remarkably accessible, especially its lunchtime concerts of popular classics. *See p 127.*

10 ★★ Statue of John Count McCormack. Ageing, unnamed statues dot the gardens, so it's a lovely contrast to see this new one of a Dublin-born hero, sculpted by Elizabeth O'Kane. McCormack

(1884–1945) was an iconic tenor, hugely successful in America where he filled Carnegie Hall and New York's Hippodrome an amazing 12 times in one season. Earning a great fortune he allegedly had a weakness for horses, and spent vast sums in backing that elusive winner.

11 ★★★ Rosarium, maze, & cascade. At the gardens' southern edge, near the Hatch Street exit, take a seat in the fragrant, recently rebuilt **Victorian rosarium**—a peaceful place to sit to seek solitude amongst cerise blooms .This was all part of the private grounds of the Earls of Iveagh, including what was the archery ground used for the International Exhibition in 1865. Most of the beauties have been restored over the years since 1955, including the **maze**, with the sundial as centerpiece. A few feet away on the western side, the vast **cascade** provides the most noise you're likely to hear in the gardens: try to get there for noon to see (and hear) it being switched on, when water thunders over the rocks.

Fountain in Iveagh Gardens.

Phoenix Park

1 Papal Cross
2 Visitors' Centre
3 Phoenix Café
4 Áras an Uachtaráin (President's Residence)
5 American Ambassador's Residence
6 Farmleigh
7 Boathouse Café
8 Sports fields
9 Dublin Zoo
10 Victorian People's Flower Garden
11 Wellington Monument

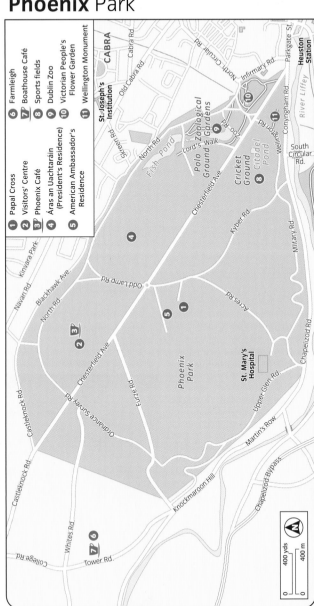

Now considered Dublin's playground, the park was originally built for the rich, with tree-lined avenues, forests, and deer roaming the grasslands. There's no significance to the mythical bird here: the Brits mispronounced its original name *Fionn Uisce* (clear water) to the more manageable 'Phoenix'. START: **Bus: 25, 51, 68 (Parkgate St.) or 37, 38 (Ashtown Gate). LUAS: Museum.** ⏱ **2–4 hr.**

① ★★ kids **Papal Cross.** The size of this white cross is awesome, stretching to a mammoth 35m (115 ft) high and weighing 40 tons. Startling in its simplicity, this was erected for Pope John Paul II's visit to give Mass on 29th September, 1979, to more than 1.25 million people (the choir alone contained 5,000 people)—around one third of the country's population. You can bet that the rest watched it live on TV. These days it's practically deserted but photos in the **Visitors' Centre** show off the Pope's gig in all its glory. Get your eyes well trained, as nearby is the area known as **Fifteen Acres,** home to hundreds of deer, descendents from Lord Ormonde's day in the 1660s (see **②**).

② ★★ kids **Visitors' Centre.** The exhibits here appeals to kids:

there's an illustrated potted history of the park from 3500 B.C. to the present, including displays of a Viking woman's grave and a rock chamber from 3500 B.C, both discovered by workers. The park was originally established as a deer park in 1662 by the Duke of Ormonde, who also loved hawking, and this display suggests the park's best places to spot deer even now. If you've already seen the Papal Cross, look for the photos upstairs of the Pope's famous Mass and the chair he sat on. Take a look at adjacent **Ashtown Castle,** a compact town house dating back to the mid-17th century. Entrance by guided tour only. ⏱ *30 min.* ☎ *01-679 1046. www.phoenixpark.ie. Free admission. Daily Mar–Sept 10am–6pm; daily Oct–Feb 10am–5pm. Bike hire daily 9:30am–5:30pm.*

Children's section in the Visitors' Centre.

The huge Papal Cross.

3 ★ **kids** **Phoenix Café.** If you haven't brought a picnic, this cafe in the Visitors' Centre's courtyard is relaxed and spacious, with decent hot food at the counter; hard to leave once you've found a sunny spot. *Visitors' Centre, Phoenix Park, Ashtown Gate.* ☎ *01-677 0090.* $.

4 ★★ **Áras an Uachtaráin (President's Residence).** It's wonderful that visitors are allowed to enter the official home of the President, Mary McAleese, the first Irish president to permit them. Originally built as a summer palace in 1751, this has been the official residence since 1938. Guided tours every Saturday take you through the State Corridor with busts of all past presidents since Douglas Hyde, and into reception rooms still used for meeting and greeting. Look up at ceilings enhanced with two French ormolu chandeliers, then down at the carpets—all handmade in Donegal, identical to those in the Vatican and the White House. In the Irish Council of State room, the stucco ceiling is gilded with 28-carat gold leaf, depicting scenes from *Aesop's Fables*. Dominating the Drawing Room with padded silk walls is a brass chandelier weighing one third of a ton. In her private office, Ms McAleese's bookcases groan with formal and personal tomes where, on my last visit, *German for Beginners* and a Slovenian phrase book were in use. Informal photos with her chums the Clintons, and a Buddha statue add to the personality of the room, so when you leave her home you feel you know

Phoenix Park: Practical Matters

Spanning 700 hectares (1,730 acres), twice the size of New York's Central Park, Phoenix Park has two separate entrances, of which Park Gate is easier to access and is right by the bicycle hire. Weekends, especially during summer, have more on offer such as sporting events, and tours of **Áras an Uachtaráin** (President's Residence) every Saturday. Officially the park is open 24 hours daily, but late-night walks are not recommended. Information: ☎ *01-677 0095. Entrances on Parkgate St. & Ashtown Gate. Park: www.phoenix park.ie. Free admission.*

The Whitehouse-like Áras an Uachtaráin.

Parliament. Incredible that even such a wealthy family often lived in a couple of rooms in winter to save on heating costs. A restaurant, cafe, and picnic tables in the gorgeous grounds give a decent array of dining options. ⏲ *1 hr. Castleknock, Phoenix Park.* ☎ *01-815 5900. www.farmleigh.ie. Free admission. Mid Mar–late Dec Tues–Sun & Bank Hol Mon. 10am–6pm; last admission 4:45pm. Tours approx every hour Thurs–Sun. Bus: 37 to Castleknock Gate.*

7 ★★ kids **Boathouse Café.** Set alongside the ornamental lake, this cafe now has altogether more modest enjoyment: coffee and paninis to give you a break, with outdoor seating to enjoy the sumptuous grounds. *Farmleigh.* ☎ *01-863 9700. Open only when House is open. $.*

the woman. ⏲ *1 hr. Tickets from Visitors' Centre. Free admission. Sat 10am–3pm.*

5 **American Ambassador's Residence.** Built in 1774 this is, unsurprisingly, closed to the public. It's still possible to peek through the huge gates to see the past residence of such luminaries as the Duke of Wellington and Sir Robert Peel.

6 ★ kids **Farmleigh.** Once home to the Guinness family, and then a state-owned VIP B&B in 2001, this 32-hectare (78-acre) opulent estate is now open for free guided tours. Hard to believe that it was originally a small Georgian house, until a succession of well-heeled Guinnesses extended it with a ballroom wing and exotic gardens. The tour shows off hallways festooned with huge portraits, 7.5m- (25 ft) high tapestries, and Venetian chandeliers, replicas of those in London's Houses of

8 ★ kids **Sports fields.** With more than 2,300 sporting fixtures every year in the park, try and catch a cricket, hurling, or even polo match in the sports fields during summer weekends. The **All Ireland Polo Club,** founded in 1873 and Europe's oldest polo club, has its home here. Sit back on a sunny Sunday and watch the 'King of Games' in all its thunderous glory, with albeit smaller crowds than a tournament in 1909 with 30,000 spectators. The cricket pitch also has a noble history, its earliest recorded match played here in 1792. **Phoenix Cricket Club,** founded in 1830, has played here from 1853 till today. John Stuart Parnell was one of its founder members, and his son Charles Stewart, famous for bringing Irish home rule to the fore (see p 24, **6**) was once their captain. The park is a little different from the days when women were only

Monkey business at Dublin Zoo.

allowed to watch from their carriages outside—thankfully anyone can take in some hurling or Gaelic football, the occasional cycle race, or even horseracing. *All Ireland Polo Club:* ☎ *01-677 6248. www.allirelandpoloclub.com. Season: May–Sept, Sat & Sun 3pm (weather permitting). Phoenix Cricket Club:* ☎ *01-677 0121. www.phoenix cricketclub.com.*

⑨ ★ kids Dublin Zoo. You might want to peep at some panthers, ogle at the elephants, or gawp at giraffes. The zoo, one of Europe's oldest, has been extended recently so the animals have more space. Even the monkeys are guaranteed to prompt squeals of excitement from the little ones. *See p 29, ⑦.*

⑩ ★★ kids Victorian People's Flower Garden. Stretching over an area of 9 hectares (22 acres), this is the place for quiet respite and peaceful walks. Laid out around 1840 and opened up in 1864 under George William Frederick Howard,

7th Earl of Carlisle, this is typical of gardens of the time with an attractive horticultural layout, ornamental lakes, and Victorian bedding schemes.

⑪ ★ kids Wellington Monument. Visible from afar, Europe's tallest obelisk at 62m (205 ft) was completed in 1861 to commemorate the victories of Dublin-born Arthur Wellesley, Duke of Wellington. Climb the stone steps at its base to admire the bronze plaques on four sides: cast from cannons captured at Waterloo, three plaques have murals representing Wellington's career, the fourth being an inscription; I especially like the *Indian Wars* by Joseph Kirk. It's also a lovely spot for catching a few rays of sun with views of the lush lawns below. If you think the monument is impressive, imagine what it would have looked like with the statue of Wellesley on horseback on the top, which was planned, but shortage of funds curtailed that idea. ●

Wellington Monument is visible for miles.

Dining Best Bets

A wall full of information at Gruel.

Best **Journey to India**
★★★ Jaipur $$$ *1 South Great George's St. (p 106)*

Best **In-Store Replenish**
★★ Avoca $$ *11–13 Suffolk St. (p 82)*

Best **Tasty Pasta**
★★ Café Bar Deli $$ *Bewley's, 78–79 Grafton St. (p 102)*

Best **Pre-Theater Meal**
★★★ Chapter One $$$$ *18–19 Parnell Square (p 103)*

Best **Hearty Soup**
★★ Gruel, $ *68A Dame St. (p 106)*

Best for **Film Buffs**
★★ IFI Café Bar $ *6 Eustace St. (p 106)*

Best **Michelin-Starred Canapés**
★★★ Thornton's $$$$$ *128 St. Stephen's Green (p 109)*

Best **Wine List**
★★ L'Ecrivain $$$$$ *109A Lower Baggot St. (p 107); and* ★★ French Paradox $$$ *53 Shelbourne Rd. (p 104)*

Best **Kids' Fun Fill-Up**
★ Wagamama $$ *South King St. (p 110)*

Best **Informal Italian**
★★ Enoteca Delle Langhe $$ *Blooms Lane (p 104) and* ★★ Dunne & Crescenzi $$ *14–16 South Frederick St. (p 103).*

Best **Coffee with a View**
★★ Bewley's Cafe $ *78–79 Grafton St. (p 102)*

Best **Splash Out for Carnivores**
★★ Shanahan's On The Green $$$$$ *119 St. Stephen's Green (p 109)*

Best **Hotel Restaurant**
★★ The Saddle Room $$$$$ *Shelbourne Hotel, 27 St. Stephen's Green (p 109)*

Best for **Sea Views**
★ Aqua $$$$ *1 West Pier, Howth. (p 102)*

Best for **Wannabe Vegetarians**
★★★ Cornucopia $$ *19 Wicklow St. (p 103); and* ★ Govindas $ *83 Middle Abbey St. (p 105).*

Best **Eccentric Pizzas**
★★ Gotham Café $$ *8 South Anne St. (p 105)*

Previous page: Elegant dining at the Winding Stair.

North Dublin Dining

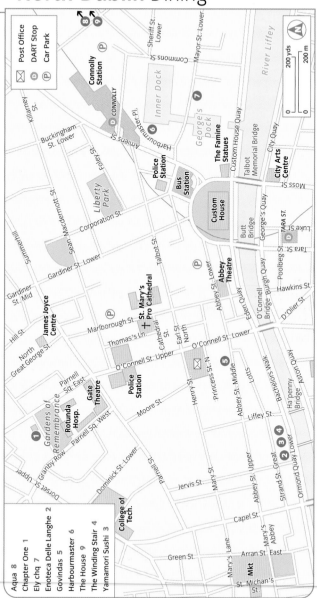

Post Office ⊠
DART Stop Ⓓ
Car Park Ⓟ

Aqua 8
Chapter One 1
Ely chq 7
Enoteca Delle Langhe 2
Govindas 5
Harbourmaster 6
The House 9
The Winding Stair 4
Yamamori Sushi 3

South Dublin Dining

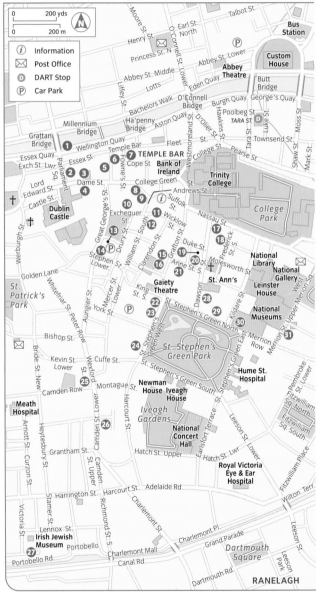

ⓘ Information
✉ Post Office
Ⓓ DART Stop
Ⓟ Car Park

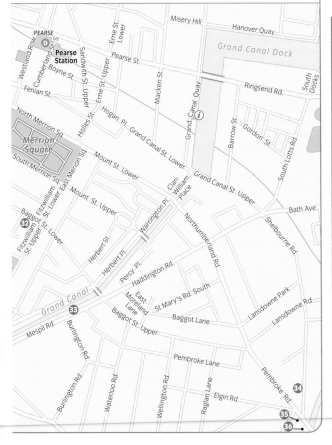

Dublin Dining A to Z

★ **Aqua** *SEAFOOD* In a renovated old sailing club out of the center, this serves top quality, fresh local seafood like lobster in garlic butter, and steamed whole sea bass, with an impressive wine list and a view to die for. *1 West Pier, Howth.* ☎ *01-832 069. www.aqua.ie. Entrees €25–€45. AE, MC, V. Lunch & dinner Tues–Sun. DART: Howth. Map p 99.*

★★ **Bentley's Oyster Bar & Grill** *SEAFOOD* This new restaurant brings seafood fans flocking to its elegant dining room for fresh Galway oysters, shellfish platters, or their famous fish soup. Good value pre-theater set menu. *22 St. Stephen's Green.* ☎ *01-638 3939. www.bentleysdublin.com. Entrees €18–€35. MC, V. Lunch & dinner daily. Map p 100.*

★★ **kids** **Bewley's** *CAFE* A Dublin legend and still gorgeous for pastries, coffee, and full Irish breakfast. Spread out with the newspaper in the upstairs dark wood interior, or enjoy the view of Grafton Street from the tiny James Joyce balcony. *78–79 Grafton St.* ☎ *01-672 7720.*

www.bewleys.com. AE, MC, V. Breakfast (from 8am), lunch & dinner daily. Map p 100.

★★ **kids** **Bobo's** *DINER* Cow-hide banquettes form the eye-catching decor in this informal American retro-style burger bar, where juicy homemade burgers stack high on tin plates. Sauces are imaginative; accompanying fries are thick-cut. Fun and good value. *22 Wexford St.* ☎ *01-400 5750. Entrees €8–€10. MC, V. Lunch daily; dinner Sun–Wed. Map p 100.*

★★ **kids** **Café Bar Deli** *MEDITERRANEAN* Sit by Harry Clarke's windows while enjoying fantastic value dining. Portions are huge, from pizzas with crisp crust to pasta full of flavor and imaginative salads. *Bewley's, 78–79 Grafton St.* ☎ *01-672 7720. www.cafebardeli.ie. Entrees €12–€15. AE, DC, MC, V. Breakfast, lunch & dinner daily. Map p 100.*

★ **Chameleon** *INDONESIAN* Sink into purple cushions for a Far Eastern experience while sampling *rijstafel*, a traditional Indonesian set meal with meat, noodles,

Eastern comfort at Chameleon.

Cornucopia's homemade savory scones.

vegetables, and seafood dishes, lightly spiced. *1 Lower Fownes St., Temple Bar.* ☎ *01-671 0362. www.chameleonrestaurant.com. Set meals €30–€40. MC, V. Dinner Tues–Sat. Map p 100.*

★★★ Chapter One *FRENCH*

The Michelin-starred haute cuisine boasts seasonal menus with select Irish fish and cured meats. Service is unfussy and friendly, with a good value pre-theater menu. Booking essential. *18–19 Parnell Square.* ☎ *01-873 2266. www.chapterone restaurant.com. Entrees €25–€40; fixed-price lunch/early-bird dinner €35, tasting menu €85. MC, V. Lunch Tues–Fri, dinner Tues–Sat. Map p 99.*

★★ Chez Max *FRENCH*

A bijou French brasserie behind Dublin Castle, complete with checked tablecloths and tiny courtyard, where you can share a platter of cheese and hams, or feast on onion soup, or rabbit stew with wholegrain mustard. *1 Palace St.* ☎ *01-633 7215. Entrees €14–€20. www.chezmax.ie. AE, MC, V. Breakfast (from 8am)* Mon–Fri; lunch & dinner daily. Map p 100.

★ Chili Club *THAI*

This tiny restaurant off Grafton Street was Dublin's first Thai eatery and remains popular. As long as you don't mind the next table at your elbow, try the decent Thai curries and spicy soups. *1 Anne's Lane.* ☎ *01-677 3721. www.chiliclub.ie. Entrees €11–€18. DC, MC, V. Lunch Mon–Fri; dinner daily. Map p 100.*

★★★ kids Cornucopia *VEGETARIAN*

This recently extended restaurant is packed every lunchtime. Line up at the counter and choose fabulous soups, crunchy salads, and hot dishes with an Asian edge. *19/20 Wicklow St.* ☎ *01-677 7583. www.cornucopia.ie. Entrees €10–€13. DC, MC, V. Breakfast Mon–Sat, lunch & early dinner daily (closes 7pm Sun). Map p 100.*

★★ Dunne & Crescenzi *ITALIAN/CAFE*

Good Italian food and wine is the hallmark here, whether a lunchtime glass of wine with crostini and pâté, or a bowl of hot linguine. Always busy. *14–16 South Frederick*

Dine in the Old Customs and Excise vaults at Ely chq.

St. ☎ 01-675 9892. www.dunneand crescenzi.com. Entrees €8–€20. MC, V. Breakfast, lunch & dinner daily. Map p 100.

★★ kids **Ely chq** MODERN EURO- PEAN   Located in the old Customs and Excise warehouse, this small chain does fabulous wine by the glass with oysters, sirloin steak, or bouillabaisse. Informal, friendly and with a huge terrace. *Customs House Quay.* ☎ 01-672 0010. www.elywine bar.ie. Entrees €15–€30. AE, MC, V. Lunch & dinner daily. Map p 99.

★★ **Enoteca Delle Langhe** ITAL- IAN   Tucked away in Quartier Bloom, this tiny rustic eatery offers hearty pasta dishes for lunch, with meat and cheese platters in the eve- nings to accompany Italian wines by the glass. Cozy sofas, or tiny out- door tables. *Blooms Lane.* ☎ 01-888 0834. Entrees €8–€15, platters €10. AE, MC, V. Lunch & dinner Mon–Sat. Map p 99.

★★ **Fallon & Byrne** MODERN FRENCH/IRISH   This large stylish space with huge windows has a sea- sonal menu, always including 28-day

aged Wexford beef, and oysters. Enjoy its 'slow food' dishes or just an upmarket burger. *11–17 Exche- quer St.* ☎ 01-472 1000. www.fallon andbyrne.com. Entrees €15–€30. AE, MC, V. Lunch daily; dinner Mon– Sat. Map p 100.

★ **The Farm** INTERNATIONAL Bright, contemporary decor of green banquettes match the eco- friendly organic dishes, ranging from Irish beef cottage pie to Asian green salad. *3 Dawson St.* ☎ 01-671 8654. www.thefarmrestaurant.ie. Entrees €15–€22. MC, V. Lunch & dinner daily. Map p 100.

★★ **Fire** MODERN EUROPEAN   A huge elaborate restaurant with fountain, sculptures, and mosaics is backed up by top cuisine, like wood- fired jumbo Tiger prawns and prime aged Irish steak. *The Mansion House, Dawson St.* ☎ 01-676 7200. www.mansionhouse.ie. Entrees €20–€30. AE, MC, V. Lunch Thurs– Sat; dinner Mon–Sat. Map p 100.

★ **French Paradox** FRENCH More like a deli serving food and wine, the Surgery Bar is loved for its

Catch the Early Bird

You could never describe Dublin as a city with good-value dining, but the good news is that it's possible to get top-dollar food at affordable prices—even more so during the tough economic times in an attempt to keep the punters coming. Look out for three-course set lunches, or pre-theater dinners (often promoted as Early Bird, Mon–Fri 5–7:30pm) at amazing prices, which might include L'Ecrivain (p 107), The Saddle Room (p 109), and Thornton's (p 109). Keep a look out for good deals on pasta or burgers at informal restaurants around Grafton Street. It's also worth checking out deals on www.toptable.com.

fine red wines with a platter of cheese, pâté, and meats, or a Camembert fondue. Upstairs, the Tasting Room is more formal. *53 Shelbourne Rd.* ☎ *01-660 4068. www.thefrench paradox.com. Entrees €12–€35; platters €10–€20. AE, MC, V. Lunch & dinner Mon–Sat. Map p 100.*

★★ kids **Gotham Café** *PIZZA* A funky interior with magazine-covered walls and small covered terrace. Pizzas come with unusual toppings (hummus or Peking duck) in a variety of sizes, always fresh and crisp, also steaks and salads. *8 South Anne St.* ☎ *01-679 5266.*

www.gothamcafe.ie. Entrees €10–€18. AE, MC, V. Breakfast, lunch & dinner daily. Map p 100.

★ kids **Govindas** *INDIAN VEGETARIAN* Good karma food in this Hare Krishna cafe is pure vegetarian and mildly spicy. Daily specials include a choice of curries, rice, and lentil dhal, as cheap as it is tasty. *83 Middle Abbey St. www.govindas.ie. Entrees €8–€10; takeout tray €7.50. MC, V. Lunch & dinner daily (closes 7pm Sun). Map p 99.*

★★ kids **Green Nineteen** *EUROPEAN* This informal new restaurant is popular thanks to reasonable

Dine with a view at IFI.

prices. Try hearty burgers or venison and root pie, or house-smoked pastrami sandwich. *19 Camden St.* ☎ *01-478 9626. www.green19.ie. Entrees €10. MC, V. Lunch & dinner daily. Map p 100.*

★★ kids **Gruel** *SOUPS* Huge tureens of soup and stews with a hunk of fresh bread make for a tasty, good-value lunch, a tad more sophisticated in the evenings. Wooden tables and a friendly, slightly shabby air make this hugely popular. *68A Dame St.* ☎ *01-670 7119. Entrees €8–€15. No credit cards. Breakfast, lunch & dinner daily. Map p 100.*

★ **Harbourmaster** *EUROPEAN* Take a seat by the open fire in the old harbormaster's office, with wood-beamed high ceilings. Food is comforting, like spicy chicken wings, and the more elaborate pan-fried scallops. *Customs House Dock, IFSC.* ☎ *01-670 1688. www.harbour master.ie. Entrees €12–€25. AE, DC, MC, V. Lunch & dinner daily (closes 7pm Sun). Map p 99.*

★ **The House** *EUROPEAN* In the pretty seaside locale of Howth, this informal bistro/cafe uses top local ingredients, so expect dishes like ham hock and potato soup, and mussels with cider and garlic. It has bare wooden tables and a simple interior, with pretty tables outside should weather permit. *4 Main St., Howth.* ☎ *01-839 6388. www.the house-howth.ie. Entrees €12–€23. MC, V. Breakfast, lunch & dinner daily. Map p 99.*

★★ kids **IFI Café Bar** *INTERNATIONAL* A peaceful oasis, this lively, high-ceilinged venue serves dishes like burgers, falafel, and spicy meatballs at bargain prices—just like their house wine. *6 Eustace St., Temple Bar.* ☎ *01-679 5744. www. irishfilm.ie. Entrees €7–€10. MC, V. Lunch & dinner daily. Map p 100.*

★★★ **Jaipur** *INDIAN* Authentic flavors and ingredients from throughout India, from Goan seafood curry to slow-cooked chicken in yogurt and cashew, with good vegetarian alternatives. Try the

Authentic Indian flavors at Jaipur.

The Lobster Pot.

Tasting Menu for a medley. Ask for a table by the window. *1 South Great George's St.* ☎ *01-677 0999. www.jaipur.ie. Entrees €15–€25. AE, MC, V. Dinner daily. Map p 100.*

★ **La Peniche** EUROPEAN   Dine aboard Dublin's only floating restaurant—with plush red seating, brass lamps, and tiny tables—on Galway Bay oysters, or steak and Guinness stew. Cruises along the river depart every Tuesday, Wednesday, and Thursday evening. *Grand Canal by Mespil Rd.* ☎ *087-790 0077. www. lapeniche.ie. Entrees €15–€19. MC, V. Lunch & dinner daily. Map p 100.*

★ **The Larder** EUROPEAN   With rugged brick walls and towering bookshelves, the friendly Larder serves hearty goodies like pan-fried duck breast, plus pancakes for weekend brunch. Popular with locals. *8 Parliament St.* ☎ *01-633 3581. www.thelarderbistro.com. Entrees €14–€22. MC, V. Breakfast, lunch & dinner daily. Map p 100.*

★★ **L'Ecrivain** FRENCH/MODERN IRISH   French haute cuisine and Michelin-starred, seasonal dishes include foie gras with cardamom and fig chutney, or West Coast lobster with basil purée, with a fantastic wine list. Good value lunch menu; advance booking essential. *109A Lower Baggot St.* ☎ *01-661 1919. www.lecrivain.com. Entrees €40–€55; tasting menu €120. Set lunch €25. AE, MC, V. Lunch Mon–Fri; dinner Mon–Sat. Map p 100.*

★ **L'Gueuleton** FRENCH   Very popular, unpretentious bistro with much-loved French onion soup, slow-roast pork belly, and other unfussy dishes, with enticing scents from the open kitchen. *1 Fade St.* ☎ *01-675 3708. www.lgueuleton. com. Entrees €15–€25. MC, V. Lunch & dinner daily. Map p 100.*

★★ **Lobster Pot** SEAFOOD   At this cozy dining room, a tray of raw fish is presented to each diner to help them order and give personal requests. Dishes of freshly caught seafood include dressed crab, sole goujons, and lobster thermidor, plus wild game in season. *9 Ballsbridge Terrace.* ☎ *01-668 0025. www.the lobsterpot.ie. Entrees €22–€34. AE, DC, MC, V. Lunch Mon–Fri; dinner Mon–Sat. Map p 100.*

★★ **Marco Pierre White Steakhouse & Grill** STEAK/SEAFOOD   Simple dishes and local ingredients mark the 'celebrity chef's' latest outing, partnering with Fitzers (the former fish restaurant). Its menu is

Charming interior of Nonna Valentina.

good value, from a starter of kipper pâté with whiskey, to mains of Irish steak (fillet, rib eye, and t-bone) and fresh fish. Great location near Grafton Street. *51 Dawson St.* ☎ *01-677 1155. www.marcopierrewhite.ie. Entrees €18–€34. AE, MC, V. Lunch & dinner daily. Map p 100.*

★ **Monty's of Kathmandu** *NEPALESE* Delicately spiced Nepalese dishes with meat and vegetarian choices plus its famous monkfish *Tareko* barbecued with spices. Try the *momos* (dumplings; 24 hours' notice needed). Weekends can be noisy. *28 Eustace St., Temple Bar.* ☎ *01-670 4911. www.montys.ie. Entrees €14–€21; tasting menu from €45. AE, MC, V. Lunch Mon–Sat; dinner daily. Map p 100.*

★ **Nonna Valentina** *ITALIAN* Overlooking swan-filled Grand Canal, dine on authentic Italian antipasto, Italian sausage with borlotti beans, or seafood tagliolini. A romantic venue with crisp white tablecloths, simple decor, and friendly service. *1–2 Portobello Rd.* ☎ *01-454 9866. www.nonnavalentina.ie. Entrees €20–€26. 3-course dinner €30. AE, MC, V. Lunch & dinner daily. Map p 100.*

★★ **Pichet** *FRENCH/ITALIAN* This is a modern take on a classic bistro, hugely popular in its first two years and still a hit. Stylishly informal, try the signature dish of crispy hen's egg wrapped in ham and deep fried. End with apple tart with butterscotch sauce. *14–15 Trinity St.* ☎ *01-677 1060. Entrees €18–€28. www.pichet restaurant.com. MC, V. Breakfast, lunch & dinner daily. Map p 100.*

★ **Pygmalion** *MODERN EUROPEAN* A perfect pit-stop in Powerscourt's dramatic atrium, this is lovely for a lunch of seasonal goodies like creamy chicken pasta and goat's cheese tart. Take a seat at the long wooden tables or a cozy sofa. *Powerscourt Centre, 59 South William St.* ☎ *01-677 9490. www.pygmalion.ie. Entrees €10–€20. MC, V. Lunch & dinner daily. Map p 100.*

★★ **Restaurant Patrick Gilbaud** *FRENCH GASTRO* Two Michelin stars means a treat in store, from Anagassin blue lobster to venison poached in mulled wine. If the (justifiably) high prices make your eyes water, try the set lunches. *21 Upper Merrion St.* ☎ *01-676 4192. www. restaurantpatrickguilbaud.ie. Entrees €50–€70. Set lunch from €38. AE,*

MC, V. Lunch & dinner Tues–Sat. Map p 100.

★ Roly's Bistro MODERN IRISH

At the bright popular dining room, handy for Lansdowne Road stadium, try beef and Guinness casserole, or the antipasti plate. Now with an adjacent cafe for breakfast and takeaways. *7 Ballsbridge Terrace.* ☎ *01-668 2611. www.rolysbistro.ie. Entrees €12–€19. AE, DC, MC, V. Breakfast, lunch & dinner daily. Map p 100.*

★★ The Saddle Room EURO-PEAN

Shelbourne Hotel's (see p 145) flagship restaurant has the elegance (and price tag) for Dublin's finest. With a marble seafood bar and gold lamé banquettes, its seasonal menus might include dishes like seafood chowder or grilled t-bone steak. Top-class service. *27 St. Stephen's Green.* ☎ *01-663 4500. www.theshelbourne.ie. Entrees €26–€42. AE, DC, MC, V. Lunch & dinner daily. Map p 100.*

★★ Shanahan's On The Green

STEAKHOUSE This American-style steakhouse with a Boston-born owner is housed in a graceful Georgian town house, with JFK's rocking-chair in the Oval Office bar. The menu will please true carnivores, with succulent t-bone, rib-eye, and fillet Angus steaks. *119 St. Stephen's Green.* ☎ *01-407 0939. www.shanahans.ie. Entrees €36–€50. AE, DC, MC, V. Lunch Fri, dinner Mon–Sat. Map p 100.*

★★ The Tea Room MODERN EUROPEAN

In U2's trendy boutique hotel, the high-ceilinged dining room with balcony serves Irish cuisine with a continental twist. Try pan-fried quail satay, rock Galway oysters with Guinness ice cream, and roasted squab pigeon. Good value set lunch. *Clarence Hotel, 6–8 Wellington Quay.* ☎ *01-407 0800. www.theclarence.ie. Entrees €28–€40. 2-course set lunch €26. AE, DC, MC, V. Lunch & dinner daily. Map p 100.*

★★ Thornton's IRISH GASTRO

Soothing decor sets the scene for dining on braised suckling pig, sautéed foie gras, or fillet of black sole. Sample the Tasting Menu (five or eight courses), or the canape taster menu in the informal lounge. *Fitzwilliam Hotel, 128 St. Stephen's Green.* ☎ *01-478 7008. www.thorntons restaurant.com. Entrees €35–€60.*

Delicate presentation at Thornton's.

Dublin's Dining Scene

Gone are the days of 'traditional Irish' overboiled cabbage and bacon; Dublin's dining scene has flourished over the last few years. And gone, too, are those that saw the Celtic Tiger as carte blanche for overpriced too-trendy-it-hurts dining, when the economic recession hit and locals saw them for what they were. Michelin stars twinkle and grow, and there's a fantastic array of multi-ethnic cuisine ranging from sushi to seafood curry. Not forgetting Irish ingredients of course. Many restaurants have turned to seasonal, locally sourced ingredients, so organic Irish spring lamb, corn-fed chicken, and line-caught sea bream are regulars on many a menu.

Tasting menus €85–€125. AE, DC, MC, V. Lunch Thurs–Sat; dinner Tues–Sat. Map p 100.

★ **Trocadero** *EUROPEAN* Famous for old-world theatrical glam, complete with curved, mirrored corridor, its deep red walls are festooned with signed photos of movie and music stars. Try deep-fried brie and roast rack of lamb, and enjoy the party—many a passing star has. *4 St. Andrew's St.* ☎ *01-677 5545. www.trocadero.ie. Entrees €16–€30. AE, DC, MC, V. Dinner Mon–Sat. Map p 100.*

★ kids **Wagamama** *JAPANESE* Fast food meets healthy eating; queue up to share long communal tables, and dive into fresh noodle soups and stir fries with Asian flavors. Fast, busy, and great for kids. *South King St.* ☎ *01-478 2152. www.wagamama.ie. Entrees €10–€16. AE, MC, V. Lunch & dinner daily. Map p 100.*

★★ **The Winding Stair** *MODERN IRISH* Huge picture windows overlooking the Liffey make this busy little dining room fresh and bright. Food is simple, like potted Kerry crab and soda bread, and pan-fried plaice with caper butter. Popular lunch spot. *40 Ormond Quay.* ☎ *01-872 7320. www.winding-stair.com. Entrees €18–€24. MC, V. Lunch daily, dinner Mon–Sat. Map p 99.*

★ kids **Yamamori Sushi** *JAPANESE* This cavernous and hugely popular restaurant is loved for its fresh sushi, sashimi, and teppanyaki at reasonable prices, plus house specials like king prawns and crab in a traditional clay pot. *38–39 Lower Ormond Quay.* ☎ *01-872 0003. www.yamamorisushi.ie . Entrees €16–€20. AE, MC, V. Lunch and dinner daily. Map p 99.* ●

Nightlife Best Bets

Best **Ornate Sculptures**
★ Café en Seine, *39 Dawson St. (p 115)*

Best **Outdoor Heated Terrace**
★★ O'Donoghue's, *15 Merrion Row (p 118)*

Best for **Relaxing Cocktails**
★ Mint Bar, *Westin Hotel, Westmoreland St. (p 117)*

Best **Cozy Suburban Local**
★★★ Kavanagh's, *1 Prospect Square, Glasnevin (p 116)*

Best **Wine Selection**
★★★ Wine Cellar, *11–17 Exchequer St. (p 118)*

Best **Old World Comfort**
★ Library Bar, *Central Hotel, Exchequer St. (p 116)*

Best **Friday Night Boogie**
★★ Anseo, *8 Camden St. Lower (p 120)*

Best **No-Nonsense Guinness**
★★ Mulligan's, *Poolbeg St. (p 118)*

Best **Bar for Rock Fans**
★★ Bruxelles, *7–8 Harry St. (p 121)*

Best **Trad Music Sessions**
★★ Cobblestone, *77 North King St. (p 122)*

Best **Brendan Behan Haunt**
★★ McDaid's, *3 Harry St. (p 117)*

Best **Artwork**
★★★ Grogans, *15 South William St. (p 115)*

Best **Camp Sunday Night**
★★ The George, *87 South Great George's St. (p 121)*

Best **Non-Guinness Stout**
★★ Porterhouse Central, *16–18 Parliament St. (p 122)*

Best **Gastro Pub**
★★★ The Schoolhouse, *2–8 Northumberland Rd (p 118)*

Best **Snug**
★★ Kehoe's, *9 South St. Anne St. (p 116)*

Best **Victoriana**
★★ Ryan's, *28 Parkgate St. (p 118)*

Most **Friendly Central Bar**
★★★ International Bar, *23 Wicklow St. (p 116)*

Best for **International DJs**
★★ POD, *Old Harcourt St. Train Station (p 119)*

Temple Bar color.

Dublin Nightlife

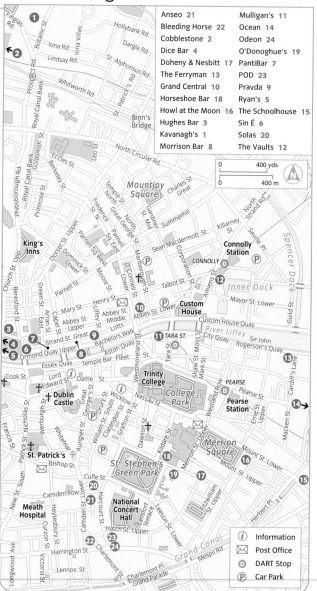

Anseo 21	Mulligan's 11
Bleeding Horse 22	Ocean 14
Cobblestone 2	Odeon 24
Dice Bar 4	O'Donoghue's 19
Doheny & Nesbitt 17	PantiBar 7
The Ferryman 13	POD 23
Grand Central 10	Pravda 9
Horseshoe Bar 18	Ryan's 5
Howl at the Moon 16	The Schoolhouse 15
Hughes Bar 3	Sin É 6
Kavanagh's 1	Solas 20
Morrison Bar 8	The Vaults 12

ⓘ	Information
✉	Post Office
Ⓓ	DART Stop
Ⓟ	Car Park

Central Dublin Nightlife

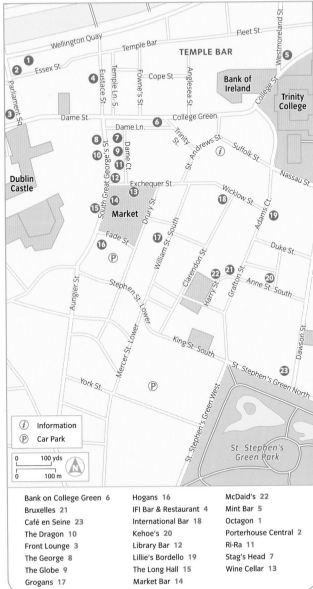

Bank on College Green **6**	Hogans **16**	McDaid's **22**
Bruxelles **21**	IFI Bar & Restaurant **4**	Mint Bar **5**
Café en Seine **23**	International Bar **18**	Octagon **1**
The Dragon **10**	Kehoe's **20**	Porterhouse Central **2**
Front Lounge **3**	Library Bar **12**	Ri-Ra **11**
The George **8**	Lillie's Bordello **19**	Stag's Head **7**
The Globe **9**	The Long Hall **15**	Wine Cellar **13**
Grogans **17**	Market Bar **14**	

Dublin Nightlife A to Z

Bars & Pubs

★ Bank on College Green

Your eyes would doubtless be dazzled by the stunning atrium in this ex-Victorian bank, with restored mosaic floor, carved stonework, and cornicing. It's on the sightseeing route, so pop in for a pint with above-average bar food. *20–22 College Green.* ☎ *01-677 0677. www.bankoncollegegreen. com. Map p 114.*

★ Café en Seine

If you like Art Nouveau balconies, erotic sculptures, murals, and marble, you'll love this staggeringly huge venue; its many little corners and niches make it seem cozy. DJ nights are packed and the food menu is reasonably priced with pies and platters to share. *39 Dawson St.* ☎ *01-677 4567. www.capitalbars.com. DJ Thurs–Sat, closes 3am. No cover charge. Map p 114.*

★ Doheny & Nesbitt

Spread over three levels, this is one of Dublin's cherished institutions, a protected building loved by local celebs (with no fuss), politicians from nearby Leinster House, and ordinary folk, with rugby memorabilia and Victorian dark-wood interior. There's a tasty selection of Irish food. *4–5 Lower Baggot St.* ☎ *01-676 2945. Map p 113.*

★ The Ferryman

One of Dublin's originals, a Georgian building in the transforming Docklands area, this was a favorite of past dockworkers. Now it's a friendly local with walls of memorabilia, old wooden advertizing boards, sport on plasma TV, and a hearty lunchtime carvery. *35 Sir John Rogerson Quay.* ☎ *01-671 7053. www.ferrymanhotel.com. Map p 113.*

★★ The Globe

With wooden floorboards and large wood tables, this spacious bar is laid-back and filled with young locals enjoying pints, coffees, free Wi-Fi, tapas, and newspapers. A DJ plays most evenings, and it merges with club Ri-Ra (see p 120). *11 South Great George's St.* ☎ *01-671 1220. www.globe.ie. Map p 114.*

★ Grand Central

This huge old banking hall has kept the gorgeous interior, with an ornate vaulted ceiling reminding me of a miniature City Hall. It attracts a fair mix of office workers, tourists, and locals, perched on bar stools at small tables, with live bands every Thursday and Saturday, and DJ on Friday nights. *10–11 O'Connell St.* ☎ *01-872 8658. www.thegrandcentral.ie. Map p 114.*

★★★ Grogans

A Dublin favorite where little has changed since 1899, you'll find yourself among left-leaning journalists, writers, and creative types. Gaze at art-covered walls, mainly by local artists, with only the

Grand Central makes fine use of an old bank.

Local art adorning Grogans.

quiet buzz of conversation as a soundtrack. You can order what food you like—as long as it's a toasted cheese sandwich. *15 South William St.* ☎ *01-677 9320. www.groganspub.ie. Map p 114.*

★★ **Hogans** This laid-back bar attracts a young bohemian crowd—not that anyone should feel out of place in this spacious and unpretentious place, with comfortable sofas in huge windows, and DJs in the refurbished basement at weekends. *35 South Great George's St.* ☎ *01-677 5904. Map p 114.*

★ **Horseshoe Bar** Designed by the late Sam Stephenson, the gem in the Shelbourne Hotel's crown has long attracted visiting celebs, local politicians, and well-heeled businessfolk, plus anyone wanting some decadence. No windows to gaze out from, just sit atop a leather stool and sip a large whiskey. *Shelbourne Hotel, 27 St. Stephen's Green.* ☎ *01-663 4500. www.theshelbourne.ie. Map p 113.*

★★ **IFI Bar & Restaurant** The Irish Film Institute is the place to escape Temple Bar's weekend partying crowd; a relaxed, unfussy space over two floors. It's ideal for a pre- or post-movie bottle of affordable house wine, pint with arty types, or an afternoon coffee (see also Chapter 6, The Best Dining, p 97). *6 Eustace St., Temple Bar.* ☎ *01-679 5744. www.irishfilm.ie. Map p 114.*

★★★ **International Bar** A friendly city center bar that feels more like your regular local, it's been run by the Donohoe family for generations. The traditional, no-frills interior with big tables and comfy seats attracts a cross-section of ages. It's also a venue for comedy and live music. (see p 128). *23 Wicklow St.* ☎ *01-677 9250. www.international-bar.com. Map p 114.*

★★★ **Kavanagh's** Better known as the Gravediggers, this family-run bar (since 1833) is adjacent to Glasnevin Cemetery, hence the nickname. To the left is the original section with dark wood snugs, far removed from a refurb. It's still charming, with lovely Guinness-quaffing locals, friendly owners, and tasty tapas. *1 Prospect Square, Glasnevin.* ☎ *01-830 7978. Map p 113.*

★★ **Kehoe's** The dark wood interior and snug (with its Victorian-era serving hatch and buzzer) has seen more than two centuries of pints being pulled. The front still has the mahogany drawers from its grocery store heritage, and upstairs is like your old auntie's living room. On summer evenings, the after-work and student crowds spill onto the pavement. *9 South St. Anne St.* ☎ *01-677 8312. Map p 114.*

★ **Library Bar** A true oasis in the midst of shopping madness, this hotel bar is all about sinking into a deep leather sofa for a warming whiskey or a morning coffee, all with a Georgian drawing-room feel. *The Central Hotel, Exchequer St.* ☎ *01-679 7302. www.centralhoteldublin.com. Map p 114.*

★ **The Long Hall** Another fine traditional bar, with little attempt to compete with the Temple Bar super-pubs (i.e. no music or TV). Yes it's long, very long and narrow, with Victorian decor: a pretty relaxing place to show up and join a real cross-section of locals. *51 South Great George's St.* ☎ *01-475 1590. Map p 114.*

★ **Market Bar** A former sausage factory inside George's Street Arcade, this vast, high-ceilinged warehouse has been carefully rede-signed with red-brick walls and sky-lights, contemporary art, and tall plants. Come for tapas and an early evening drink leading to buzzing evenings. There's a large heated courtyard and Wi-Fi throughout. *Fade St.* ☎ *01-613 9094. www. marketbar.ie. Map p 114.*

★★ **McDaid's** This classic old Dublin boozer poured many a pint for literary legends Brendan Behan and Thomas Kavanagh. Losing noth-ing of its charm, its welcoming Vic-torian dark wood walls pack locals, students, and visitors into its tiny space. Try for a snug, or perch up at the bar for a friendly chat. *3 Harry St.* ☎ *01-679 4395. Map p 114.*

Behan's fave watering hole, McDaid's.

★ **Mint Bar** A sophisticated cocktail bar in the Westin Hotel's basement, this is suitable for a quiet intimate drink, probably at the end of a long night. There's also a decent food menu. *The Westin Hotel, Westmoreland St.* ☎ *01-645 1000. www.westin.com/dublin. Map p 114.*

★★ **Morrison Bar** Part of the John Rocha-designed hotel, this Liffeyside Northsider is a chic place

The former sausage factory and now Market Bar.

to start an evening out. Sink onto comfortable leather couches and choose from its extensive cocktail list. *The Morrison, Ormond Quay.* ☎ *01-887 2400. www.morrison hotel.ie. Map p 113.*

★★ **Mulligan's** Reputed to serve the best Guinness in town since the 1850s (even though James Joyce, a regular, had characters in *Dubliners* drinking hot whiskeys). Mulligan's is for those who appreciate a smooth pint, ornate dusty mirrors, and mahogany snugs immersed in old-time ambience. *Poolbeg St.* ☎ *01-677 5582. www.mulligans.ie. Map p 113.*

★ **Ocean** Tucked away on Grand Canal Quay, this is frequented by hip, Dockland-residing twenty-somethings. Join them on a summer's evening on a comfy sofa by the window, or on the waterfront terrace. Decent brunch, dinner, and finger-food menu. *1st floor, Millennium Tower, Charlotte Quay Dock.* ☎ *01-668 8862. www.oceanbar.ie. Map p 113.*

★ **Octagon** Many come here hoping to spot the hotel's owners, and yes, Bono used to pop by (rarely). An eight-sided snug interior with skylight, it's relatively quiet even when filled with wannabe celebs and rich businessfolk sipping pricey cocktails. Not the place to order a pint; try its elaborate 'creations'. *Clarence Hotel, 6–8 Wellington Quay.* ☎ *01-407 0800. www. theclarence.ie. Map p 114.*

★ **Odeon** Once part of the old Harcourt Street Railway Station, it now boasts a huge patio and Art Deco interior. Popular with young folk en route to the adjacent Tripod (see p 119), or post-work crowd relaxing with decent wine and food, there are regular music and weekend club nights. Service can be slow. *Harcourt St.* ☎ *01-478 2088. www.odeon.ie. Map p 113.*

★★ **O'Donoghue's** Tourists love where musicians The Dubliners made their name, it's also busy with office workers who pack into the large heated alleyway. With walls lined with photos of music stars of the past, it's still a place for nightly trad music sessions. *15 Merrion Row.* ☎ *01-660 7194. www. odonoghues.ie. Map p 113.*

★★ **Ryan's** The likes of Presidents Clinton, Kennedy, and Bush Sr have supped pints here: a true Victorian boozer with mahogany fittings and old lamps. It's retained the charm of the one-time gentleman's retreat; luckily more egalitarian these days. *28 Parkgate St.* ☎ *01-677 6097. www.fxbrestaurants.com. Map p 113.*

★★★ **The Schoolhouse** Part of the Schoolhouse hotel (see p 145), its 12m (40 ft) beamed ceilings, deep sofas, and log fires are a treat on a cold evening—although it's rather like having a tipple in a cavernous church. Informal and lively after work, its food is a real hit, and the garden is a lovely spot in summer. *2–8 Northumberland Rd.* ☎ *01-614 4733. www.schoolhouse.ie. Map p 113.*

★ **Stag's Head** Tucked away from the main drag, the eponymous head stares down from the wall. The decor is Victoriana with Connemara marble-inlaid bar and stained-glass windows. Its homey ambience means you'll feel cocooned in here with a decent pint, with an affable mix of students, IFSC workers, and afternoon skivers. Live traditional music every Thursday to Sunday. *1 Dame Court.* ☎ *01-679 3687. www.thestagshead.ie. Map p 114.*

★★★ **Wine Cellar** In the stone-walled basement of Fallon & Byrne (see p 81 & p 104), more than 700 bottles of wine from 12 countries are on offer with decent food

Drinking lessons at The Schoolhouse.

(oysters and fish stew) to soak it up. Comfortable and cozy yet reasonably priced, especially on Happy Mondays with only €1 corkage on any bottle bought. A real find. *11–17 Exchequer St.* ☎ *01-472 1010.* www.fallonandbyrne.com. Map p 114.

Clubs

★ **Howl at the Moon** Four bars spread over four floors draw in a young crowd, with DJs playing popular dance tracks. Check out each area, from 'the Hoity Toity Bar' on the top floor, one level with cozy sofas and bar stools, to the heated outdoor terrace. No cover or dress code. *Lower Mount St.* ☎ *01-634 5460.* www.capitalbars.com. *No cover charge. Wed–Sat till late. Map p 113.*

★ **Lillie's Bordello** With its red walls and sensual decor, this was once *the* place to be seen by the glam set: now it's filled with wannabe celebs and a fair share of poseurs. Non-members stand a better chance of getting in earlier in the week, when entrance is free. *Adam Court, Grafton St.* ☎ *01-679 9204.* www.lilliesbordello.ie. *Free Sun–Tues, Wed €5, Thurs €10, Fri & Sat €15. Map p 114.*

★★ **POD** Leaping into action in 1993, the old railway station is now a music Mecca. Garage and house ring out especially on club nights at Tripod with noted resident DJs, plus occasional high-caliber guest DJs like Paul Oakenfold and John Digweed. (For live music see also *Crawdaddy*, p 130.) *Old Harcourt St. Train Station.* ☎ *01-476 3374.* www.pod.ie. *Wed–Sat from 11pm–2:30am. Cover from €10. LUAS: Harcourt Street. Map p 113.*

The Wine Cellar.

★★ Ri-Ra The Globe's (see p 115) dark, cozy basement has nightly DJs playing, depending on the night, a range of R&B, 80s, electro, and rock. A chilled-out crowd with a general carefree, pose-free attitude. *Dame Court.* ☎ *01-671 1220. www. rira.ie. Mon–Sat 11pm–2:30am. No cover charge. Map p 114.*

★ The Vaults The basement of Connolly Station houses 19th-century vaults, and the stone-walled venue with spooky statues is now split off into several bar and club areas. The Nite Club is for serious 20-something techno fans, or just enjoy a quiet glass of wine in the main bar in the early evening with city slickers. *Harbourmaster Place, IFSC.* ☎ *01-605 4700. www.the vaults.ie. Cover from €5, depending on DJs. Map p 113.*

DJ Bars

★★ Anseo Pronounced An-Shaw, this slightly left-field, casually hip, and fun place has DJs playing at weekends. Although there's no 'official' dance space, those in the mood will get up and boogie where it takes their fancy. *8 Camden St. Lower.* ☎ *01-475 1321. No cover charge. Map p 113.*

★ Bleeding Horse A huge, rambling old bar (the original horse allegedly staggered by in 1649) split over three floors, DJs play on Friday and Saturday nights: old favorites for singing along to, rather than needing space to dance. Snug corners and small balconies provide space to chat (yell) above the music. *25 Camden St.* ☎ *01-475 2705. No cover charge. Map p 113.*

★★ Dice Bar Resembling a Goth hangout, DJs at this black-walled, red-lit bar play an eclectic mix, like rockabilly, blues, and occasional Frank Zappa nights. With no cover charge, the 'dance floor' can get

crowded. A worthy Northsider venue. *79 Queen St.* ☎ *01-872 8622. www.thatsitdublin.com. No cover charge. Map p 113.*

★ Pravda With its bizarre Russian-themed decor (murals and knick-knacks) and a world of vodkas, Pravda's live music nights get the twenty-something punters in, and weekends have good DJs playing indie. Plus its famous King Kong Club on Thursdays. Competition is tight for the fabulous red leather sofas upstairs. *Lower Liffey St.* ☎ *01-874 0090. www.pravda.ie. No cover charge. Map p 113.*

★★ Sin É This friendly, studenty pub on the Liffey has a loyal following. Relatively new yet with a well-worn, comfortable feel, it's pretty relaxed during the week with board games and pub food, upping the tempo at weekends with live bands and DJs. Good fun. *14–15 Upper Ormond Quay.* ☎ *01-878 7078. www.thatsitdublin.com. No cover charge. Map p 113.*

Flying spacemen at the Dice Bar.

Glam decor at The Dragon.

★ **Solas**   Resident DJs spin diverse club nights, with a fondness for jazz-funk, and top cocktails and the roof-top terrace have made this a popular hangout. There's also a decent menu plus a pizza menu till 3am. *31 Wexford St.* ☎ *01-478 0583. www.solasbars.com. No cover charge. Map p 113.*

Gay Bars & Clubs

★ **The Dragon**   Featuring camp snugs on one side, elaborate glam lighting, and Asian-styled decor, DJs at this dedicated gay club play techno, hard house, and pop most nights. The friendly, snappy-dressed crowd love the cocktails (try the Cookie Monster) and flirting galore in the outdoor smoking area. *South Great George's St.* ☎ *01-478 1590. www.capitalbars.com. No cover charge. Map p 114.*

★ **Front Lounge**   This large, gay-friendly bar is as stylish as they come; all designer suits and sleek seating, with stylish artwork on the walls. Tuesday is the highlight when the coiffed hair comes down for April Showers' Casting Couch karaoke. *33 Parliament St.* ☎ *01-670 4112. No cover charge. Map p 114.*

★★ **The George**   An institution in Dublin's gay community, this longstanding favorite (The Dragon's big sister) is split into two: the Old Bar is frequented by pint-drinking men of all ages, and the adjacent Dance Bar/Club attracts a young crowd, with weekend DJs, Wednesday's comedy nights and Shirley's Bingo Sundays. *87 South Great George's St.* ☎ *01-478 2983. www.capitalbars.com. No cover charge. Map p 114.*

★★ **PantiBar**   Owned by adored drag queen Ms Panti herself, this is more than just a bar: regular events like Monday's craft evenings, DJs playing the best party tunes, and Thursday's drag show have made it a firm favorite in the gay-friendly world. The comfortable interior, with a basement, is adorned with funky event posters. *7–8 Capel St.* ☎ *01-8740 710. www.pantibar.com. No cover charge. Map p 113.*

Live Music Bars (see also Chapter 8, The Best Arts & Entertainment p 123)

★★ **Bruxelles**   A rock venue for bikers and late birds, live bands play five nights a week, mainly rock, indie, and blues. Its three bars have two DJs playing rock and indie at weekends, best experienced with a Belgian beer. The patio is popular

Original brewing tools at Porterhouse Central.

on summer evenings. *7–8 Harry St.* ☎ *01-677 5362. No cover charge. Map p 114.*

★★ Cobblestone   Ignore the shabby-looking exterior; this is probably the best place to hang out with locals listening to good Irish music. Informal sessions take place most evenings and weekends, with

Live trad at Cobblestone.

scheduled gigs in the back room. It's great fun, friendly, and earthy. *77 North King St, Smithfield.* ☎ *01-872 1799. Live music Mon–Wed 9pm; Thurs–Sat 7pm; Sun 2pm. No cover charge. LUAS: Smithfield. Map p 113.*

★ Hughes Bar   A little rough round the edges (even though it's just behind the Four Courts), this is renowned for some of the finest trad Irish with musicians pitching up for a session. There are good sounds nightly from around 9:30pm, with a haphazard selection of fiddles and pipes. *19 Chancery St.* ☎ *01-872 6540. No cover charge. Map p 113.*

★★ Porterhouse Central   No Guinness served here, as this three-floored venue is the flagship of the huge microbrewery chain. Live bands play nightly on a tiny stage (best seen from the balcony) with bluesy rock, local bands, and traditional music sessions. Look out for the huge brass brewing pot on the top floor. *16–18 Parliament St.* ☎ *01-679 8847. www.porterhouse brewco.com. No cover charge. Map p 114.* ●

Arts & Entertainment Best Bets

Best for **Swinging Your Partners**
★★ Comhaltas Ceoltoiri Eireann, *32 Belgrave Square, Monkstown* (p 129)

Best **Experimental Dance**
★ Project Arts Centre, *39 East Essex St. Temple Bar* (p 134)

Best **Sporting Crowds**
★★★ Croke Park, *Jones's Rd* (p 131), and ★★ Aviva Stadium. *62 Lansdowne Rd* (p 131)

Best for **Race Goers**
★★ Leopardstown Racecourse, *Leopardstown* (p 132)

Best for **the Blues**
★★ J. J. Smyth's, *12 Aungier St.* (p 130)

Best **Beckett Plays**
★★ Gate Theatre, *1 Cavendish Row* (p 133)

Best **Concert Acoustics**
★★ National Concert Hall, *Earlsfort Terrace* (p 127)

Best **Pub Comedy**
★★★ The International, *23 Wicklow St.* (p 128)

Best **Specialist Kids' Venue**
★★ Ark, *11a Eustace St., Temple Bar* (p 127)

Best **Songs Among Sculptures**
★★ Dublin City Gallery, The Hugh Lane, *Parnell Square North* (p 127)

Best for **Arthouse Movies**
★★ IFI, *6 Eustace St.* (p 129)

Best **Dramatic Architecture**
★★ Grand Canal Theatre, *Grand Canal Square* (p 133)

Best for **Mega Gigs**
★★ The O2, *North Wall Quay* (p 131)

Best **Daytime Drama**
★★★ Bewley's Cafe Theatre, *78–79 Grafton St.* (p 133)

Best **Karaoke**
★★ The Village, *26 Wexford St.* (p 131)

Best for **a Flutter on the Dogs**
★★ Shelbourne Park, *Shelbourne Park* (p 132)

Best **Venue for Young Local Bands**
★★ Whelan's, *25 Wexford St.* (p 131)

Racing on the flat at Leopardstown.

Previous page: Violins on display, Dublin.

North Dublin

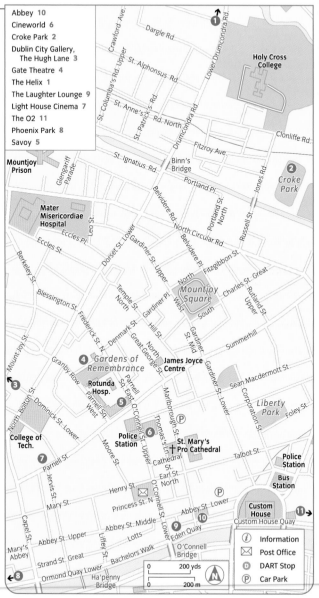

South Dublin

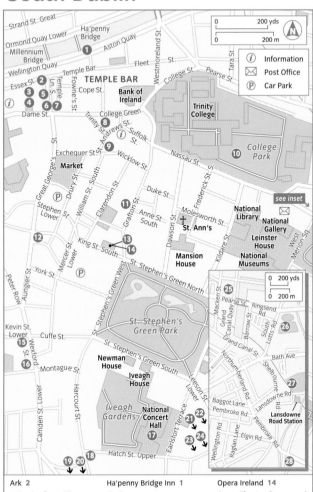

Ark 2	Ha'penny Bridge Inn 1	Opera Ireland 14
Aviva Stadium 27	IFI 5	Opera Theatre Company 6
Bankers 8	The International 9	Pavilion 23
Bewley's Café Theatre 11	JJ Smyth's 12	Project Arts Centre 3
Button Factory 7	Lambert Puppet Theatre 21	RDS 28
Comhaltas Ceoltoiri Eireann 22	Leopardstown Racecourse 24	Shelbourne Park 26
CrawDaddy 18	Marlay Park 19	University of Dublin Cricket Club 10
Gaiety Theatre 13	Mill Theatre 20	The Village 15
Grand Canal Theatre 25	National Concert Hall 17	Whelan's 16
	Olympia Theatre 4	

Arts & Entertainment **A to Z**

Children's Entertainment

★★ Ark   The lovely Children's Cultural Centre hosts programs, shows, festivals, and exhibitions for kids of all ages, with artists and performers from Ireland and around the world. Most events are held during summer months, and weekends year-round. *11A Eustace St, Temple Bar.* ☎ *01-670 7788. www.ark.ie. Tickets free–€10. Map p 126.*

★★ Lambert Puppet Theatre   This family-run theater uses handmade puppets for fairy-tales like *Jack and the Beanstalk* and edgier stories like Oscar Wilde's *The Selfish Giant.* Performances are held most weekends, suitable especially for ages 4 to 9. *Clifton Lane, Monkstown.* ☎ *01-280 0974. www.lambertpuppet theatre.com. Tickets €10–€13. DART: Salthill & Monkstown. Map p 126.*

Classical Music & Opera

★★ Dublin City Gallery, The Hugh Lane   This gorgeous gallery

hosts **Sundays at Noon,** free recitals in the Sculpture Gallery with specially commissioned works, concerts coinciding with major exhibitions, and visiting international performers. Concerts are informal, free, and attract all ages. *See p 125,* ❷.

★★ National Concert Hall   Sitting on the edge of Iveagh Gardens, the purpose-built hall is one of Ireland's best for live performances. The resident RTÉ National Symphony Orchestra gives weekly recitals, with concerts every night and most lunchtimes, by Irish and international artists. Its year-round program takes in grand opera, star soloists, and world-class orchestras. See p 91, ❾. *Earlsfort Terrace.* ☎ *01-417 0000. www.nch.ie. Tickets €10–€60. Map p 126.*

★ Opera Ireland   Performing four operas in winter and spring seasons at the **Gaiety Theatre**, Opera Ireland puts on classics by Donizetti, Mozart and the like, but

Performance at the National Concert Hall.

Advance Tickets & Listings

For the latest concert, theater, cinema, and event listings, pick up a copy of **The Ticket** (www.ireland.com/theticket) a weekly guide free with Friday's **Irish Times**. Venues around Temple Bar have free copies of fortnightly **The Event Guide** (www.eventguide.ie) and look out in bars and cafes for the tabloid-sized **Totally Dublin** and magazine **InDublin** (www.indublin.ie), both free. Buy tickets from **Tickets. ie** (☎ 087-263 3920; www.tickets.ie), **Ticketmaster** (St. Stephen's Green Shopping Centre; www.ticketmaster.ie), **Celtic Note** (see p 85) (Nassau St.), **Centra Temple Bar** (45–46 Wellington Quay), **Dublin Tourism** (Suffolk St.), and **Ticketron** (Jervis St. Shopping Centre and Stephen's Green Shopping Centre).

is also renowned for its Irish premieres of contemporary opera. Past seasons have seen top names such as Pavarotti, Carreras, and Domingo as guest soloists. ☎ 01-478 6041. www.operaireland.com. Tickets €25–€120. See p 126.

★ Opera Theatre Company

Operating on a small budget, this friendly crew has toured the country since 1986 performing in venues ranging from theaters to castles, like Mozart's The Marriage Of Figaro at Trinity College in 2010. As well as the classics, it also performs new operas by Irish composers. *Office: Temple Bar Music Centre, Curved St. ☎ 01-679 4962. www.opera.ie. Prices depend on the venue. Map p 126.*

Comedy

★ **Bankers** This cozy basement in a city center bar hosts hit-and-miss **Stand-Up at the Bankers** with resident improv troupe the Craic Pack on Fridays, and Irish comics every Saturday. Avoid the front row seats unless you don't mind being picked on. *16 Trinity St. ☎ 01-679 3697. www.bankerscomedyclub. com. Doors open 9pm; show 9:30pm. Tickets €10. Map p 126.*

★ **Ha'penny Bridge Inn** This popular quayside bar puts on varied entertainment every night. Tuesday's open-mic night **Battle of the Axe** sees all sorts put themselves in the firing line of the discerning public, while Thursday is comedy night, with stand-up, improv, and sketch. *42 Wellington Quay, Temple Bar. ☎ 086-8115 6987. www.battle oftheaxe.com. Doors open 9pm; show 9:30pm. Tickets €9. Map p 126.*

★★★ The International

Upstairs at this friendly bar sees improv or stand-up comedy every night, with resident MCs Aidan Bishop and Des Bishop. The laughs come courtesy of some of Ireland's hottest talent at my personal favorite venue. Jazz bands play downstairs on Tuesdays and Thursdays. *23 Wicklow St. ☎ 01-679 3697. www.theinternationalcomedyclub. com. Doors open 8:30pm; show 9pm. Tickets €10; Sun €5. Map p 126.*

★ **The Laughter Lounge** This slick venue hosts well-established stand-up acts every Thursday to Saturday, with four comedians from Ireland and overseas. Snacks or a three-course meal are available before the show, and DJs and late bars keep the party going long after the chuckles die down. *Basement, 4–8 Eden Quay.* ☎ *01-878 3003. www.laughterlounge.com. Doors open 7pm; show 8:30–11pm. Tickets €25–€30. Map p 125.*

Irish Traditional Music & Dance

★★ Comhaltas Ceoltoiri Eireann
This national cultural center promotes Irish traditional music, with regular music and dance sessions in a variety of venues. Try and get to a ceilidh, with caller, musicians, and dancers who know their sets from their steps and jigs. Its main branch hosts sessions every Tuesday (beginners) and Wednesday (everyone). Forget *Riverdance*, just jump in. *32 Belgrave Square, Monkstown.* ☎ *01-280 0295. www.comhaltas.ie. Most events are free. DART: Seapoint. Map p 126.*

Movies

★ Cineworld
One of the largest and most popular movie theaters in the city center, with 17 large

Comedy improv at The International.

screens, comfortable seats, and a host of refreshments including a licensed bar. Most movies are new releases and blockbusters, plus the occasional Bollywood and kung-fu flick, a fabulous place for a 3D experience. *Parnell St.* ☎ *1520-880 444. www.cineworld.ie. Tickets €6.30–€10.40. Map p 125.*

★★ IFI
Newly refurbished, the Irish Film Institute screens arthouse, foreign, and vintage movies, as well as housing the Irish Film Archive, a shop, and library. Several movies are screened daily, plus annual Polish, German, and French film festivals. *6 Eustace St.* ☎ *01-679 5744. www.ifi.ie. Tickets €7.75–€9.20. Map p 126.*

★★ Light House Cinema
It's all about the best Irish, independent, and arthouse films at Dublin's newest cinema. Sleek, minimalist design and multi-colored seating helps make it a contemporary cultural experience. *Market Sq, Smithfield.* ☎ *01-879 7601. www.lighthousecinema.ie. Tickets €9. Map p 125.*

★ Savoy
Dublin's oldest movie theater has been screening since 1929. It's seen countless changes, and is now a slick, six-screen venue. A €2m refurbishment restored the original interior features, and the marble-floored foyer and chandeliers make it the location of choice for many film festivals. *17 Upper O'Connell St.* ☎ *0818-221 122. www.omniplex.ie. Tickets €7–€9. Map p 125.*

Pop, Rock & Jazz

★★ Button Factory
Previously known as Temple Bar Music Factory, and now refurbished, this well-worn venue has live bands most nights Wednesday to Saturday, ranging from international names to local bands. There's a large balcony, new

Dublin's Cultural Year

All things turn green for the week-long St. Patrick's Day revelry, with parades galore and ample liquid refreshment (around 17th March; www.stpatricksfestival.ie). Following that is the more sedate **Handel's Messiah Festival** on the anniversary of its world premiere (13th April). Contemporary dancers from around the world take to various venues during the **Dublin Dance Festival** in April or May (☎ 01-679 0524; www.dublindancefestival.ie). Usually held in May, gay contributors to the theater, past and present, are showcased in the **Dublin Gay Theatre Festival** (www.gaytheatre. ie). Majestic tall ships come sailing by in June's **Docklands Maritime Festival** (☎ 01-818 3300; www.dublindocklands.ie), and Phoenix Park hosts the vibrant **Bloom In The Park** (☎ 01-668 5155; www.bloom inthepark.com). From June, **Temple Bar**'s cultural edge is spotlighted during the summer's plethora of festivals (☎ 01-677 2255; www.templebar.ie) from outdoor film screenings to live opera. Head for the coast and Dún Laoghaire's **Festival of World Culture** in August. International music, theater, and cabaret crams into a frantic fortnight in September's **Dublin Fringe Festival** (☎ 01-677 8511; www.fringefest.com), followed by the **Dublin Theatre Festival** (☎ 01-677 8439; www.dublintheatre festival.com), the world's oldest English-speaking festival.

bar, and seating with a stage view. *Curved St., Temple Bar. ☎ 01-670 9202. www.buttonfactory.ie. Most tickets via City Discs (next door); please see Advance Tickets & Listings p 128. Map p 126.*

★★ **CrawDaddy** This 300-capacity live music venue (part of the huge POD) hosts an eclectic range of performers most nights. Spread over two floors, the balcony has reserved seating, with standing (and dancing) on the first floor. With excellent acoustics and lighting, recent performers include Black Eyed Peas and Lee Perry. Enjoy a relaxed pre-gig drink at the adjacent Lobby Bar. (See also *POD*, p 119.) *Old Harcourt Station, Harcourt St. ☎ 01-662 4305. www.pod.ie. Cover from approx €10. Map p 126.*

★★ **J.J. Smyth's** The football might be on to entertain Guinness-supping locals, but upstairs at this cozy local, evenings see jazz (Thursdays) and blues (Thursday to Saturday) at this much-loved music venue, highly regarded by musicians. *12 Aungier St. ☎ 01-475 2565. www.jjsmyths.com. Music from 10pm. Entrance approx €10. Map p 126.*

★ **Marlay Park** A huge suburban park spanning over 121 hectares (300 acres), and summertime venue to supergroups likely to attract around 30,000 fans. In 2009, Metallica and Fatboy Slim did just that. Tickets (at varying prices dependent on the group) via agencies in advance. *Marlay Park, Rathfarnham. www.mcd.ie/venues. Map p 126.*

★★ **The O2** Ireland's mega venue, the rebuilt Point Theatre, is run by the Live Nation entertainment company. Huge international names appear at the 14,000-capacity arena, or the 2,000-seater theater, recently hosting smash-hit musical *We Will Rock You* from London's West End. *North Wall Quay.* ☎ *01-819 8888. www.theo2.ie. Prices vary depending on the event. Shuttle buses from city center; LUAS: The Point. Map p 125.*

★ **Olympia Theatre** This one-time music hall now offers its ornate space to the occasional play, but more often big names (albeit safe bets) in the music scene such as Chris Rea and Lyle Lovett. Look out for the gorgeous 19th-century stained-glass canopy outside, finally repaired in 2007. *72 Dame St.* ☎ *01-679 3323. www.mcd.ie/venues. Prices vary depending on the performer. Map p 126.*

★ **RDS** The Royal Dublin Society, founded in 1731, is now a multi-purpose venue hosting concerts,

The Olympia Theatre's stained glass canopy.

shows, and the Horse of the Year Show. 2010 acts include Pink and the Irish Chamber Orchestra. *Ballsbridge.* ☎ *01-668 0866. www.rds.ie. Prices vary depending on the event. Map p 126.*

★★ **The Village** On the floor above the spacious, comfortable bar, bands play nightly, with a small balcony (created in 2009) overlooking the stage. Not just local groups; Fairport Convention has played here. Sundays see the popular rock-and-roll karaoke **Songs of Praise.** *26 Wexford St.* ☎ *01-475 8555. www.thevillagevenue.com. Tickets: around €10. Map p 126.*

★★ **Whelan's** A sociable wooden-floored bar over two floors sees a live band every night in the back room, showcasing Irish talent plus international stars, including folk, rock, and indie (Nick Cave and Mike Mills have played here). It's a winning combination, and recent extensions indicate its popularity. Look out for the Stone Man statue! *25 Wexford St.* ☎ *01-478 0766. www.whelanslive.com. Cover charge for gigs varies. Map p 126.*

Spectator Sports

★★ **Aviva Stadium** The new name for Lansdowne Road stadium, after a huge expansion and rebuilding, now with a 50,000 capacity. Reopened for international football (soccer) and rugby from early 2010, it's a piece of astounding hi-tech architecture, as well as providing an unbeatable atmosphere. *62 Lansdowne Rd.* ☎ *01-238 2300. www.avivastadium.ie. Tickets from www.ticketmaster.ie. From €30 upwards. Map p 126.*

★★★ kids **Croke Park** Local sporting culture at its best, either at a hurling or Gaelic football match at this 80,000-seat stadium, known as the Croker. Partisan yet

Cheering on the 'Dubs' at Croke Park.

non-segregated stands mean a good-natured, high-octane day out. *Jones's Rd.* ☎ *01-865 8657. Season Apr–Sept. Tickets from www.ticket master.ie., www.gaa.ie., www. crokepark.ie. Admission: €10–€40. Map p 125.*

★★ Leopardstown Racecourse Built in 1888, this suburban racecourse is one of Europe's best, with year-round racing over flat and national hunt courses. Racing experts will appreciate the history; names in the Hall of Fame include Pat Eddery and Nijinsky. *Foxrock.* ☎ *01-289 0500. www. leopardstown.com. Admission: €15–€30. LUAS: Sandyford. Map p 126.*

★★ Phoenix Park This mammoth urban park has a long history of sports fields, and summer weekends are best to see them in full flow. Try and get to see a polo match. *(See Chapter 5, The Best of the Outdoors). Map p 125.*

★★ Shelbourne Park Speedy greyhounds provide a fun and cheap night out in an easily accessible stadium. Study the form, although it's more luck than skill that brings winnings. Weekends are livelier, with crowds flocking for the Irish Greyhound Derby in September. *Shelbourne Park.* ☎ *01-668 3502. www.igb.ie. Races Wed, Thurs & Sat night from 7pm. Admission: €10. Map p 126.*

★★ University of Dublin Cricket Club Trinity College's picturesque cricket ground has the 'Pav' bar on the boundary, and sunny summer weekends bring student spectators out in force. The club has several teams, including women's teams. *See p 39,* **9**. *Trinity College, College Green.* ☎ *01-896 1000. Season Apr–Aug. Map p 126.*

Let off the leash at Shelbourne Park.

Family-friendly entertainment at Bewleys Theatre Café.

Theaters & Venues

Abbey Founded in 1903 by W.B. Yeats, Ireland's adored theater went bankrupt in 2004, but new management and redesign means it's still going strong, performing classics like *Macbeth*. **The Peacock**, under the Abbey's foyer, is a bijou venue for new plays and contemporary classic drama. The theater is due to move to the Docklands in 2012. *26 Lower Abbey St.* ☎ *01-878 7222. www.abbeytheatre.ie. Ticket prices vary. Map p 125.*

★★★ Bewley's Cafe Theatre

A play, a bowl of soup, and a small audience at wooden tables; this charming venue in the old Oriental Room hosts lunchtime drama plus occasional evening comedy and jazz. Perfect to drop by between shopping or sightseeing. *78–79 Grafton St.* ☎ *086 878 4001. www. bewleyscafetheatre.com. Ticket €15 inc. light lunch. Map p 126.*

★ Gaiety Theatre

Dublin's long-established theater doesn't choose high-brow dramatics these days. After major refurbishment, it hosts mega-musicals and sell-out shows such as *Riverdance* plus London West End musicals like *Joseph* and *Blood Brothers*. **Opera Ireland** also performs here. *South King St.* ☎ *01-677 1717. www.gaietytheatre.ie. Tickets €22–€55. Map p 126.*

★★ Gate Theatre

A Dublin landmark (both architecturally and theatrically) this opulent building opened as an avant-garde theater in 1928. With longstanding connections to Samuel Beckett and Brian Friel, it participates in many international festivals. The new €6m wing, completed in 2008, has a huge flexible rehearsal space. *1 Cavendish Row.* ☎ *01-874 4045. www.gate theatre.ie. Tickets €20–€35. Map p 125.*

★★ Grand Canal Theatre

Designed by Daniel Libeskind and part of Docklands' transformation, this futuristic 2,100-capacity theater opened in March 2010 with the Bolshoi Ballet's *Swan Lake*. The stage is purpose-built to withstand heavy

Projects Arts Centre in Temple Bar.

weights—including the ¾-ton car fly-ing across the stage in *Chitty Chitty Bang Bang*. Look for year-round musicals, big-name gigs, and pro-ductions on a grand scale. *Grand Canal Square* ☎ *01-677 7999. www.grandcanaltheatre.ie. Tickets from €30 depending on the show. Map p 126.*

★ **The Helix** This contemporary theater in Dublin College Universi-ty's campus has shown productions ranging from *Swan Lake* by Moscow City Ballet to Ibsen's *A Doll's House*, plus regular children's shows. *DCU, Collins Ave, Glasnevin.* ☎ *01-700 7000. www.thehelix.ie. Tickets €10–€50. Bus: 4, 11, 13. Map p 125.*

★ **Mill Theatre** This 220-seater theater, opened in 2006, is part of mega-mall Dundrum Town Centre. Its year-round program is filled with contemporary productions by Irish, American, and British companies, plus amateur theater groups, chil-dren's shows, and music events. *Dundrum Town Centre.* ☎ *01-296 9340. www.milltheatre.com. Tickets €10–€20. LUAS: Balally. Map p 126.*

★ **Pavilion** Out in coastal Dún Laoghaire (see p 152), this hosts the Festival of World Cultures and Dub-lin Theatre Festival. A bright space with excellent bar and restaurant, it has a busy year-round schedule with touring companies, plus ballet and contemporary dance. *Marine Rd.* ☎ *01-231 2929. www.pavilion theatre.ie. Tickets €10–€30. DART: Dún Laoghaire. Map p 126.*

★ **Project Arts Centre** Temple Bar's cultural jewel, Project show-cases contemporary dance, theater, and visual arts mainly with Irish art-ists. Sticking to its principles of nur-turing emerging talent—U2 and Neil Jordan started out here—come for experimental works rather than blockbuster classics. Its upstairs bar appeals to an eclectic arty crowd. *39 East Essex St., Temple Bar.* ☎ *01-881 9613. www.project.ie. Map p 126.* ●

Lodging Best Bets

Best **Wow-Factor Lounge**
★★★ Number 31 $$$$ *31 Leeson Close* (p 144)

Best **Value for Families**
★★ Bewley's $$ *Merrion Rd, Ballsbridge* (p 140)

Best **Hip Boutique Hotel**
★★★ Dylan $$$$$ *Eastmoreland Place* (p 141)

Best **Hedonists' Party Pad**
★ The Clarence $$$$ *6–8 Wellington Quay* (p 140)

Best **In-House Art Gallery**
★★ Merrion Hotel $$$$ *Upper Merrion St.* (p 143)

Best for **Scholarly Sleeping**
★★ Trinity College $$ *College Green* (p 146)

Most **Dramatic Approach**
★★ Clontarf Castle Hotel $$$ *Castle Ave* (p 141)

Best **Dublin Treasure**
★★ The Shelbourne $$$$$ *27 St. Stephen's Green* (p 145)

Best **Value Northsider**
★★ Maldron Hotel $$$ *Smithfield Village* (p 143)

Best **Suburban Luxury**
★★★ Four Seasons $$$$$ *Simmonscourt Rd, Ballsbridge* (p 141)

Best **Cheap Apartment**
★★ Kingfisher $$ *166 Parnell St.* (p 143)

Best **Design Chic**
★★ Morrison Hotel $$$$$ *Ormond Quay* (p 144)

Best **Value Penthouse**
★★ Molesworth Court $$ *Schoolhouse Lane* (p 144)

The colorful entrance to Bewley's.

Best **Garden Terrace View**
★★ Fitzwilliam $$$$ *St. Stephen's Green* (p 141)

Best **Temple Bar Cheapie**
★★ Harding Hotel $$ *Copper Alley, Fishamble St.* (p 143)

Best **Live Music**
★★ The Westbury $$$$$ *Grafton St.* (p 146)

Best **Use of a Bank**
★★ Westin $$$$ *College Green, Westmoreland St.* (p 146)

Best **Historic Landmark**
★★ The Gresham $$$$ *23 Upper O'Connell St.* (p 142)

Previous page: Elegant frontage of Browne's Townhouse.

North Dublin Lodging

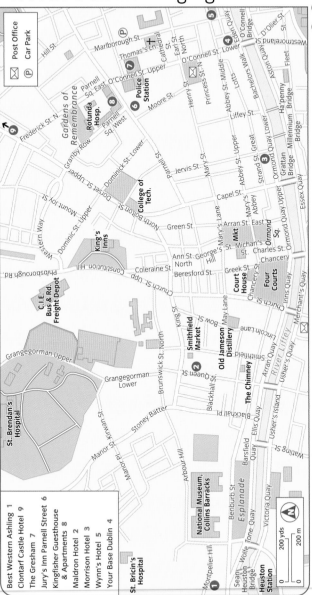

☒ Post Office
Ⓟ Car Park

Best Western Ashling 1
Clontarf Castle Hotel 9
The Gresham 7
Jury's Inn Parnell Street 6
Kingfisher Guesthouse
& Apartments 8
Maldron Hotel 2
Morrison Hotel 3
Wynn's Hotel 5
Your Base Dublin 4

South Dublin Lodging

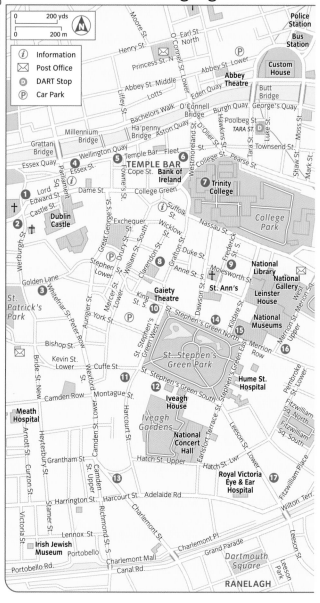

Legend:
- ⓘ Information
- ✉ Post Office
- Ⓓ DART Stop
- Ⓟ Car Park

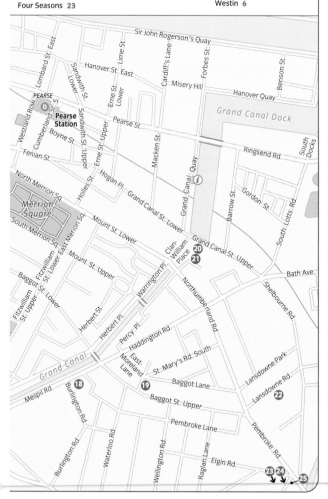

Dublin Lodging A to Z

★★ Ballsbridge Towers Part of the D4 Hotels group, the spacious unfussy rooms offer good value, complete with huge bed, writing desk, and armchairs. South of the center in suburban Ballsbridge, it's well connected with the DART and Aircoach. *Pembroke Rd.* ☎ *01-668 4468. www.d4hotels.ie. Doubles €69–€149 w/ breakfast. AE, MC, V. Map p 139.*

★ Bentley's Town House This 18th-century town house is now a Georgian boutique hotel (previously known as Browne's) with 11 rooms with items of original furniture mixed with contemporary extras. Rooms are on the small side, with the best view overlooking St. Stephen's Green. *22 St. Stephen's Green.* ☎ *01-638 3939. www.bentleysdublin.com. 11 units. Doubles €120–€200 w/ breakfast. AE, DC, MC, V. Map p 139.*

★ kids Best Western Ashling Clean, park-side rooms at decent prices, a short walk from the city center but next to the tram stop for the O2. Recently renovated rooms are spacious; conference and meeting rooms, plus complimentary Wi-Fi will appeal to the business traveler. *Parkgate St.* ☎ *01-677 2324. www.ashlinghotel.ie. 225 units. Doubles €80–€155 w/breakfast AE, DC, MC, V. Map p 137.*

★★ Bewley's This striking 1800s Masonic building offers great value for families, with the same rates per room throughout the year. Safely and predictably furnished, all rooms have double and single beds; ask for a room with a tower view. It's a short bus ride into town. *Merrion Rd, Ballsbridge.* ☎ *01-668 1111. www.bewleyshotels.com. 304 units. Doubles €89 w/breakfast. AE, DC, MC, V. Map p 139.*

★★ Camden Court Hotel Close to the city center, on a busy shopping street, comfortable guestrooms are simply furnished in strong colors. Quieter rooms overlook the courtyard, and there are large family rooms. Leisure facilities include a swimming pool, sauna, and gym. Good value. *Lower Camden St.* ☎ *01-475 9666. www.camdencourthotel.com. 246 units. Doubles €99–€165 w/breakfast. AE, DC, MC, V. LUAS: Harcourt. Map p 139.*

★ The Clarence Owned by U2's lead singer, Bono, this hotel is understated elegance rather than rock-star exuberance, with oak furniture and unfussy furnishings. Some rooms have a Liffey view and balcony—although it can be noisy. A complete rebuilding is planned for

'Subject to Availability'

During popular events like international rugby matches, major pop concerts, and St. Patrick's Day, prices leap up and availability down, so bear this in mind if your dates are flexible. The flip side is that luxury hotels often have good deals during off-peak times, especially at weekends, particularly via their own websites. Wherever you intend staying and whenever you visit, it's worth booking as far ahead as possible.

The Clarence.

2012. *6–8 Wellington Quay.* ☎ *01-407 0800. www.theclarence.ie. 49 units. Doubles €130–€250. AE, DC, MC, V. Map p 139.*

★★ Clontarf Castle Hotel

Carved stone lions and suits of armor greet you at this former castle, nowadays a mix of original stone walls with contemporary glass. Utterly romantic (especially the deep red-toned Presidential Suite), this suburban spot is close to Dublin Bay. *Castle Ave.* ☎ *01-833 2321. www.clontarfcastle. com. 111 units. Doubles €89–€189 w/ breakfast. AE, MC, V. Map p 137.*

★★★ Dylan

With deep red carpets, gilded silver mirrors, and designed headboards that should be in an art gallery, this new five-star boutique hotel was built in a former Victorian nurses' home. Oozing style, luxuries include top Frette linens, iPod docking stations, and Italian marble bathrooms. *Eastmoreland Place.* ☎ *01-660 3000. www.dylan.ie. 44 units. Doubles from €179. AE, DC, MC, V. Map p 139.*

★ kids Eliza Lodge

With a guesthouse feel and friendly service, rooms are simple and light; some of them rather small and most with a Liffey view. It's worth paying a little extra for the Penthouse room with balcony and huge bay windows. It

can get noisy. *23/24 Wellington Quay.* ☎ *01-671 8044. www.dublin lodge.com. 18 units. Doubles from €86. AE, MC, V. Map p 139.*

★★ kids Fitzwilliam

This hip Conran-designed luxury hotel has large, contemporary rooms. Overlooking St. Stephen's Green, garden terrace suites have balconies with heated lamps. The bijou 24-hour gym and nail bar are loved by trendy families and business travelers. *St. Stephen's Green.* ☎ *01-478 7000. www.fitzwilliamhoteldublin. com. 139 units. Doubles €165–€350. AE, DC, MC, V. Map p 139.*

★★★ Four Seasons

In a peaceful suburban area, this huge hotel with stunning exterior offers all the usual Four Seasons excellence. Rooms are classic and well furnished, and ornate carpets and contemporary artwork set the tone in the imposing foyer. There's a decent spa with pool, plus spacious lounges and terraces. *Simmonscourt Rd, Ballsbridge.* ☎ *01-665 4000. www. fourseasons.com/dublin. 197 units. Doubles €165–€445. AE, DC, MC, V. Map p 139.*

★★ kids Grand Canal Hotel

The hotel is a short walk to the city center and the Aviva Stadium, and overlooks the canal. Well-furnished,

Getting the Best Rate

There isn't much point in quoting a 'rack rate' in this chapter (the hotels' published price); instead, it's more useful to put the commonly available minimum price for a standard double, ranged with the hotel's own 'standard' price. You'll rarely have to pay the rack rate at top hotels if booking in advance, and only when you request a specific date will you get a price. For the best discounts at top hotels, check their own websites, as they often offer good discounts and packages especially in low season, at weekends, and away from major events (see 'Subject to Availability'). It's also worth checking out discounts at booking websites like **www.hotels.com** and **www.booking.com**; that luxury top-notch hotel might actually be more affordable. In most instances, the cheapest rates do not include breakfast.

comfortable rooms are spacious and quiet, with extras such as free Wi-Fi and tea- and coffee-making facilities. Balcony rooms boast amazing views. *Grand Canal Street Upper.* ☎ *01-646 1000. www.grandcanal hotel.com. 142 units. Doubles €80– €230. AE, DC, MC, V. Map p 139.*

★★ **The Gresham** An O'Connell Street landmark since 1817, the irregular-sized rooms all have understated elegance with plasma TV and free Wi-Fi. Or you can splash out on the opulent Elizabeth Taylor Suite. Triple-glazing helps keep the street noise out. *23 Upper O'Connell St.* ☎ *01-874 6881. www.gresham-hotels.com. 288*

The Boutique style Dylan Hotel.

units. Doubles €125–€350. AE, DC, MC, V. Map p 137.

★★ **kids** **Harding Hotel** On Dublin's oldest street, near Temple Bar's party scene (noisy at weekends), this is a good budget choice. The decent-sized simple rooms all have fridge, kettle, small TV, and free Wi-Fi, with large triple and family rooms. *Copper Alley, Fishamble St.* ☎ *01-679 6500. www.harding hotel.ie. 52 units. Doubles €100–€125 w/breakfast. AE, MC, V. Map p 139.*

★ **kids** **Herbert Park** In a peaceful suburb by a huge park, it's close to Aviva Stadium and the RDS. Large, elegant rooms are light and contemporary, and for a little extra, executive rooms overlook the park with a kids' playground. Breakfast is wonderful; parking costs extra. *Ballsbridge.* ☎ *01-667 2200. www.herbert parkhotel.ie. 153 units. Doubles €90–€200. AE, DC, MC, V. Map p 139.*

★ **kids** **Jury's Inn Christchurch** Straightforward, simple rooms bang opposite the cathedral make this ideal for sightseeing if not for a quiet night (request upper floors at the back for peace; front for views). Rates are for room only, so it's a good deal for families (sleeps two kids). *Christchurch Place.* ☎ *01-454 0000. www.jurysinns.com. 182 units. Rooms €59–€160. AE, DC, MC, V. Map p 139.*

★ **kids** **Jury's Inn Parnell Street** Similar rooms and style to the Jury's Inn Christchurch (suits families; see above) this is just off the north end of O'Connell Street, so quieter at night. It also has a small fitness area and a 24-hour coffee bar. *Moore St. Plaza, Parnell St.* ☎ *01-878 4900. www. jurysinns.com. 253 units. Doubles €59–€160. AE, DC, MC, V. Map p 137.*

★★ **kids** **Kingfisher Guesthouse & Apartments** A simple, decent budget option, just off O'Connell

Sink into the drawing room at the Merrion.

Street, most rooms have a tiny kitchenette with microwave and fridge. The apartments (three separate locations) are great value, with living room and kitchen for roughly the same price. *Guesthouse: 166 Parnell St.* ☎ *01-872 8732. www. kingfisherdublin.com. 32 units (inc guesthouse & apartments). Doubles €90–€110, apartment €55 per person. AE, MC, V. Map p 137.*

★★ **kids** **Maldron Hotel** Previously known as Comfort Inn, on a large cobbled square, the unfussy rooms have bathtub, power shower, and free broadband. Most rooms have a double and single bed; suites also available. (Also at Cardiff Lane.) *Smithfield.* ☎ *01-485 0900. www. maldronhotels.com. 92 units. Doubles €79–€210. AE, DC, MC, V. Map p 137.*

★★ **Merrion Hotel** Gorgeous Georgian luxury recreated from elegant town houses—including the

Morrison Hotel's Georgian suite.

Duke of Wellington's birthplace—guestrooms have the finest linen, antiques, and high sash windows. Walls are laden with 19th- and 20th-century art, and contemporary pleasures include an infinity pool in the Tethra Spa. *Upper Merrion St.* ☎ *01-603 0600. www.merrionhotel.com. 143 units. Doubles €199–€450. AE, DC, MC, V. Map p 139.*

★ **kids Mespil Hotel** Located on peaceful Grand Canal, standard rooms in this huge hotel are bright and simple, most having a double and single bed. It's good value for families, or party-goers happy with a short walk home. *Mespil Rd.* ☎ *01-488 4600. www.mespilhotel.com. 255 units. Doubles €105–€205. AE, DC, MC, V. Map p 139.*

★★ **Molesworth Court** The selection of luxury apartments includes a three-bedroom penthouse suite sleeping six, good value especially given the huge wraparound balcony, sauna, and fully equipped kitchen/living area. Bang in the middle of the sightseeing trail, it's nonetheless down a peaceful side street. Clean, contemporary, and bright. *Schoolhouse Lane.* ☎ *01-676 4799. www.molesworthcourt.ie. 4 units.*

Suites €180–€420. MC, V. Map p 139.

★★ **Morrison Hotel** One of Dublin's coolest designer hotels, all rooms and the lobby are Zen-like with an Oriental feel courtesy of John Rocha. It's all about relaxing, with dimly lit corridors, huge mirrors, and tasteful artwork in the lobby. It's worth paying extra for the larger executive rooms. *Ormond Quay.* ☎ *01-887 2400. www.morrison hotel.ie. 138 units. Doubles €120–€340. AE, DC, MC, V. Map p 137.*

★★★ **Number 31** Converted Georgian houses meet modernist mews, with sumptuous decor, courtesy of the late architect Sam Stephenson. The contemporary sunken lounge sets the scene, and each uniquely shaped room has stylish, strong colors. Guests adore the breakfasts—all homemade dishes. *31 Leeson Close.* ☎ *01-676 5011. www.number31.ie. 21 units. Doubles €150–€320 w/breakfast. AE, DC, MC, V. Map p 139.*

★ **O'Callaghan Stephen's Green Hotel** One of several in the chain, this is a decent mid-range choice, renovated and extended in 2009. Rooms are simple and stylish in dark wood, some with a small terrace. Its lobby area is busy and bright, with a contemporary atrium. *St. Stephen's Green.* ☎ *01-607 3600. www.ocallaghanhotels.com. 99 units. Doubles €75–€235. AE, DC, MC, V. Map p 139.*

★★ Radisson Blu Royal Hotel

A luxury hotel opened in 2007 in a quiet corner of the city center. Decent-sized rooms are elegant and have wonderful power showers in the bathrooms. Executive rooms have access to the huge roof terrace; extensive meeting and conference facilities. *Golden Lane.* ☎ *01-898 2900. www.radissonblu.ie/royalhotel dublin. 150 units. Doubles €150–€190. AE, DC, MC, V. Map p 139.*

★ Schoolhouse Hotel

Set in an 1850s school, with turrets and stone archways like a Gothic church, this small, friendly hotel has simple, bright rooms. It's a 20-minute walk into town, so its Grand Canal location suits those seeking a quiet break. *2–8 Northumberland Rd.* ☎ *01-667 5014. www.schoolhousehotel.com. 31*

units. Doubles €129–€199 w/breakfast. AE, DC, MC, V. Map p 139.

★★ The Shelbourne

The grande dame of Dublin hotels, recently refurbished, still attracts local dignitaries. Most of the original features remain, from the Waterford chandelier and marble lobby to the traditional ambience of rooms, yet with modern comforts. The original rooms overlook St. Stephen's Green. Rooms are larger than those in the new wing. *27 St. Stephen's Green.* ☎ *01-663 4599. www.theshelbourne.ie. 265 units. Doubles €235–€355. AE, DC, MC, V. Map p 139.*

★ Staunton's on the Green

One of the better value Georgian guesthouses, and former home of Henry Grattan Guinness, (grandson of Arthur), this guesthouse has a private entrance into tranquil Iveagh Gardens. Refurbished rooms are modern in light wood, and the lounge's period furniture and open fire is welcoming. *83 St. Stephen's Green South.* ☎ *01-478 2300. www. stauntonsonthegreen.ie. 57 units.*

A touch of glam at The Shelbourne.

The Westin's huge Atrium.

Doubles €100–€165 w/breakfast. AE, MC, V. Map p 139.

★★ **Trinity College** Summer vacation sees great deals in students' accommodation blocks at this historic establishment. Single and twin rooms rather than doubles, most units have two rooms sharing private bathroom, lounge, and kitchen. Great for families or small groups. *Trinity College Accommodation Office, College Green.* ☎ *01-896 1177. www.tcd.ie. 700 units. From €60 per person. Available mid-Jun–late Sept. MC, V. Map p 139.*

★★ **The Westbury** Grafton Street's only hotel is still a local institution. This five-star has spacious, modern rooms with handmade Irish furniture, plus everything from beauty salons to boardrooms. Save time for afternoon tea in the gallery accompanied by a pianist. *Grafton St.* ☎ *01-679 1122. www.doylecollection. com. 205 units. Doubles €200–€400. AE, DC, MC, V. Map p 139.*

★★ **Westin** Built in the 1860s and a bank until 1998, this listed building retains its banking theme with original vaults now housing the basement Mint Bar. Rooms are ornate and plush, with ultra-comfy beds and marble bathrooms, some overlooking the five-floor glass atrium. Triple-glazed windows ensure a quiet night. *College Green, Westmoreland St.* ☎ *01-645 1000. www.westin.com/dublin. 163 units. Doubles €135–€400. AE, DC, MC, V. Map p 139.*

★★ **Wynn's Hotel** Wynn's has been around since 1845—check out the plaque marking Pádraic Pearse's meeting in 1913. Rooms have a fresh look since refurbishment, with lovely dark wood furniture and writing desks. Ask for a quieter room at the back or upper floors. Friendly and decent value, the family rooms are a good size. *35–39 Lower Abbey St.* ☎ *01-874 5131. www.wynns hotel.ie. 65 units. Doubles €99–€175. AE, DC, MC, V. Map p 137.*

★ **Your Base Dublin** Fully furnished, serviced apartments are primarily for long-stay business guests, with a minimum three-night stay. With a handful of separate venues, this top-floor choice has Liffey views from floor-to-ceiling windows, large living rooms, and fully-equipped kitchens. *Your Base at Aston Quay Dublin, Aston Quay. Booking* ☎ *01-814 7000. www.abodedublin. com. 12 properties (assorted locations). 1-bedroom apartment from €90/night. AE, MC, V. Map p 137.* ●

Your Base Dublin Apartment.

Powerscourt House & Gardens

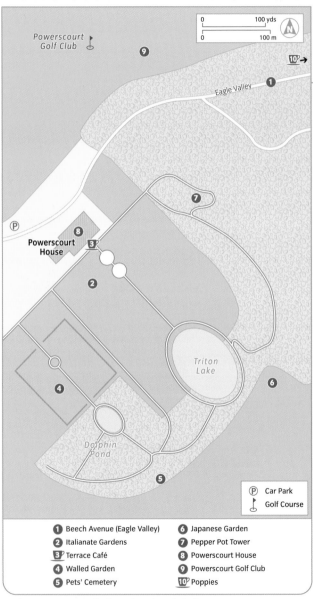

0	100 yds
0	100 m

Powerscourt Golf Club

9

10 →

Eagle Valley **1**

Powerscourt House

P

8

3

2

7

Triton Lake

6

4

Dolphin Pond

5

P	Car Park
🏌	Golf Course

1 Beech Avenue (Eagle Valley)	**6**	Japanese Garden
2 Italianate Gardens	**7**	Pepper Pot Tower
3 Terrace Café	**8**	Powerscourt House
4 Walled Garden	**9**	Powerscourt Golf Club
5 Pets' Cemetery	**10**	Poppies

Previous page: Boats to Ireland's Eye leave from the harbor.

In the shadow of **Big Sugar Loaf Mountain in Wicklow,** the estate's highlight is undoubtedly its formal gardens. The house has altered greatly over time; originally a 14th-century castle, it was rebuilt by Richard Wingfield and his ancestors from 1603, and gutted by fire in 1974. The newly restored house is imposing, but the statue-studded lawns and secluded pathways are the real jewels. START: **See box, Practical Matters.**

Marble mosaics at the Italianate Gardens.

❶ ★★ Beech Avenue (Eagle Valley) The 'getting there' really is half the fun. This tranquil walk from Enniskerry takes you along the milelong avenue lined by more than 2,000 beech trees. (My last visit was on a sunny October day when the leaves were a vibrant red.) There's barely a car in sight, and few signs to reassure you that yes, you are on the right road. Enjoy your first glimpse of the Wicklow Mountains on your left as you approach the house.

❷ ★★ Italianate Gardens. This grandiose section of the grounds was commissioned by the sixth Viscount Powerscourt in the 1840s, and designed by architect Daniel Robertson, a proponent of Italianate gardens. Suffering from gout, Robertson allegedly directed operations to the 100 workers from a wheelbarrow, while fortified by a bottle of sherry. When the bottle ran out, work ended for the day. Thankfully it all paid off. Your best views are from the upper terrace, guiding your eyes down the mosaic patterned staircase with pebbles from nearby Bray, past 6th-century statues of Apollo, Diana, and Cupid, vases copied from Versailles, and dazzling green lawns with deep red rose beds. At the bottom, a pair of life-size winged Pegasus horses made from zinc that guard the lilyfilled Triton pond are framed perfectly by the landscaped slopes and the 501m (1,644ft) high peak of Big Sugar Loaf.

Pagoda and bridge in the Japanese Garden.

3 kids **Terrace Cafe.** Take your Mediterranean tarts, Irish bread, or homemade cakes onto the terrace, for the jaw-dropping panorama of the Wicklow Mountains and the upper terrace. ☎ *01-204 6070. $.*

4 ★ **Walled Garden.** Dating back to 1740, this is one of Powerscourt's oldest features. As you enter through the elaborate Chorus Gates decorated with bugling angels, the aroma of the fragrant rose beds will waft over. Look out for the memorial to Julia, 7th Viscountess Powerscourt, who died in 1931. She obviously had a thing for da Vinci and the like, as her fountain is embellished with four busts of great Italian masters.

5 kids ★★★ **Pets' Cemetery.** Powerscourt's owners become more endearing at this resting place for the much-loved animals of the Wingfield (past owners) and Slazenger (current) families. Pay your respects to Sailor, the curly retriever and faithful companion for five years (died 1909); Tommy, a Shetland pony who died in 1936 aged 32, and his companion Magic; and the Jersey cow Eugenie who had 17 calves and produced over 100,000 gallons of milk. It's not unusual for beloved

Practical Matters: Powerscourt

Organized bus trips from Dublin drop you at the gates, but it's more fun (and cheaper) on public transport. Catch the DART to coastal Bray (40 min; for basic transport information see also *Dún Laoghaire*, p 152), and then bus no. 185 to Enniskerry village from outside the station (15 min). It's approximately a 1½ mile walk, from the village and turning right along Eagle Valley, to the main entrance of the gardens. Open daily 9:30am to 5:30pm; gardens close at dusk in winter. Admission: €8 adults; €7 concs; €5 children 15 and under, under 5s free. ☎ 01-204 6000. www.powerscourt.ie

pets to be buried in marked graves in Ireland, but this is thought to be the country's largest private pets' cemetery.

6 ★★ Japanese Garden. Laid out half a century after the Italianate Gardens (**2**), and built on reclaimed bogland, take the concentric paths leading to dazzling red Japanese maples and tiny bridges over the stream. It's very much a European vision of an Oriental style, but comes pretty close, complete with Chinese fortune palms and pagoda, and as a whole representing the discovery of our inner souls. Nearby, look out for the 18th-century grotto with water cascading over fossilized sphagnum moss, found on the banks of the River Dargle.

7 ★ Pepper Pot Tower. The eastern section of the gardens is dominated by the fairytale-like tower which rises from the surrounding conifers, built to commemorate the Prince of Wales's 1911 visit. Shaped like the 8th Viscount's pepper pot, you can climb to the top for views of the grounds. Follow in the footsteps

Powerscourt House.

of the Viscount and stroll through the surrounding woodland, known as his 'private walk and American Garden' because of the rare plants from North America.

8 ★ Powerscourt House. It's hard to match the outstanding vistas and collection of gardens, so the recently restored house might be a bit of a disappointment. Home to a stylish shopping gallery (mainly with Irish interior designs of Avoca), the historic ballroom has been restored and is now a prestigious venue for society weddings and dinners. Inside the house, an exhibition has photographs showing the history of the building, and how the entrance hall once looked before the fire, complete with antlers, stucco ceiling, and cluttered with Victorian furniture. On Sundays, the ballroom is open to the public (unless there's a private party), wonderful if only for the golf-course views from its windows.

9 ★ Powerscourt Golf Club. Visitors can play a round at the estate's two championship courses. The East Course, opened in 1996 and designed by Peter McEvoy, was the venue of the 1998 Irish PGA Championship. The newer West Course opened in 2003, and both share stunning scenic views. ☎ *01-204 6033. Tee times summer: 8am–7pm; winter 8am–3pm. Visitors €65 per round, inc lunch in the clubhouse. Club hire €40. Advanced booking advisable.*

10 Poppies. Walk back to Enniskerry, and head to this cozy bistro with cheerful checked tablecloths creating a homey feel, serving homemade dishes like homity pie and rhubarb crumble. *The Square, Enniskerry.* ☎ *01-282 8869. www.poppies.ie. $.*

Dún Laoghaire to Dalkey

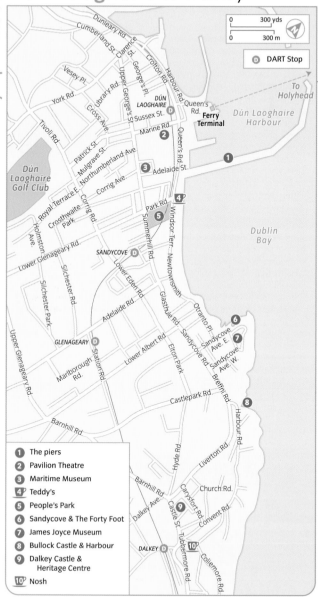

0   300 yds
0   300 m

D DART Stop

1. The piers
2. Pavilion Theatre
3. Maritime Museum
4. Teddy's
5. People's Park
6. Sandycove & The Forty Foot
7. James Joyce Museum
8. Bullock Castle & Harbour
9. Dalkey Castle & Heritage Centre
10. Nosh

ormerly known as Kingstown, in honor of King George IV's visit, the port town of Dún Laoghaire is a popular day trip. It's a bracing coastal walk from here to Sandycove for seal-spotting or even a swim, and on to swanky suburb Dalkey. The hardy can continue to Killiney's golden beaches, or if you don't fancy the walk, Dún Laoghaire alone is a great day out, especially at weekends. START: **DART to Dún Laoghaire.**

Dun Laoghaire pier.

❶ ★★ **The piers.** The west and east piers, popular promenading spots, jut out among the yachts, fishing boats, and huge Holyhead passenger ferry. A touch of sunshine brings everyone onto the walkways, with families, roller-bladers, and joggers striding out. If you return here at the end of the day, the place is likely to be packed.

❷ ★ kids **Pavilion Theatre.** This seafront cultural center has all manner of entertainment, from kids' drama festivals and concerts to high-brow theater. If you're staying in the town for the evening, it's well worth checking out their program of events. *Marine Rd.* ☎ *01-231 2929. www.paviliontheatre.ie.*

❸ ★ kids **Maritime Museum.** Due to reopen by early 2011 after major refurbishment, the museum's home is the **Mariners' Church** built in 1837, one of the last remaining sailors' churches. The collection hosts a staggering 7,000 artifacts including the 200-year-old Bantry Boat captured during the French invasion, the Baily Optic from Howth's lighthouse, plus Victorian stained-glass windows. Climb the Bell Tower for spectacular harbor views. *Haigh Terr. www.mii.connect.ie.*

❹ kids **Teddy's.** Going strong since 1957, Ireland's adored ice-cream shop has them queuing down the road for the house favorite—a 99 flake (ice cream in a cone with a flakey chocolate bar). There's also a huge choice of candies, the sort you haven't seen since childhood. *1A Windsor Terrace.* ☎ *01-284 5128. $.*

❺ ★ **People's Park.** Near the town center, the park comes to life on Sundays for the **Farmers' Market** (a relatively new concept in Dublin). Cheeses, bread, cakes, and fruit stalls lie between hot food, crafts, and gifts. Good for grabbing a dish of freshly made couscous or stocking up for a picnic (weather permitting). *Market: Sun 10am–5pm.*

Farmers Market in People's Park.

6 ★★ **Sandycove & The Forty Foot.** This tiny cove of golden sand is a haven for families and anyone seeking precious sun so not surprisingly it's packed during warm weekends. The historic Forty Foot, once a 'Gentleman's bathing place' (i.e. nude) now accepts women swimmers. A chilly dip even in summer, this is the venue of the Christmas

Day swim for the truly hardy. Look for the signs indicating the seal preservation area, and what to do if one comes swimming by, which is basically look but don't touch.

7 **James Joyce Museum.** Easy to spot from your walk, the sturdy Martello Tower—one of many along Ireland's east coast built to withstand Napoleonic invasions—now houses the James Joyce Museum. The novelist wrote and set his opening episode of *Ulysses* here, when our hero Leopold Bloom starts out inside 'a Martello Tower in Sandycove' on 16th June. Celebrations for the tome, known as Bloomsday, kick off every year on that day from here. The tiny museum houses Joyce's personal possessions and rare editions of the cherished novel. Ascend to the gun platform, also described in *Ulysses*, for sweeping sea views. ⏱ *40 min. Joyce Tower, Sandycove.* ☎ *01-280 9265. Admission: €7 adults, €6 (concs). Mar–Oct: Mon–Sat 10am –1pm and 2–5pm, Sun & p/hols 2–6pm, Nov–Feb by arrangement only.*

8 ★★ **Bullock Castle & Harbour.** Now owned by Carmelite Sisters, the castle was once inhabited

Practical Matters: Dún Laoghaire

Located 12km (8 miles) south of Dublin, Dún Laoghaire is easily accessed by the speedy DART train. Jump on at Connolly, Tara Street, Pearse, or Grand Canal Dock stations, with a single ticket for €2.30. Services run approximately every 10 to 15 minutes Monday to Saturday (6:15am–midnight); every 30 minutes Sunday (9am–midnight). Info line ☎ 1850-366 222; 24-hour talking timetable: ☎ 1890-77 88 99. The **Tourist Information Office** (www.dlr tourism.com) is located at the Dún Laoghaire Ferry Terminal, open Monday to Saturday 10am to 12:45pm and 2pm to 6pm; closed Sunday.

Swimmers brave the cold as the sunsets at Sandycove.

by monks who charged fishermen a quota of fish they caught on the open seas. Without payment, they wouldn't be allowed back in the harbor. These days the tiny Bullock Harbour, with tame seals bobbing between the boats, has no such fishy taxes, not even from the two small rental stalls with 5m (16ft) fishing boats for hire. ID is required, and those with no sailing experience will get a quick demonstration of how to use the engine. Fishing gear is also for hire to try your hand at catching mackerel or codling. *Boat hire: 2 on Bullock Harbour (unnamed);* ☎ *01-280 6517;* ☎ *01-280 0915. Late May–mid Sept. €30/hr sailing; €20/hr fishing. Rods: €8/session. Daily, dawn–dusk.*

9 ★ **kids** **Dalkey Castle & Heritage Centre.** Near Dalkey's center is the castle, and a visit here covers a 14th-century town house and a 10th-century church and graveyard. Introductory tours of the castle include The Medieval Experience, with an experienced guide dressed up as an archer, cook, or Viking coin minter, giving an entertaining historical flavor to the medieval world. ⏱ *1 hr. Castle St, Dalkey.* ☎ *01-285 8366. www.dalkeycastle.com. €6 adults, €5 concs, €4 children. Mon*

& Tues–Fri 9:30am–5pm; Sat, Sun & p/hols 11am–5pm. Costumed guides May–Oct.

10 **Nosh.** A super place to end the day, whether with a Bloody Mary, roast guinea fowl, or good old fish 'n' chips. Small, cozy, very popular, and oozing Dalkey style. *111 Coliemore Road, Dalkey.* ☎ *01-284 0666. $$.*

Bullock Harbour.

Howth

1. Farmers' Market
2. St. Mary's Abbey
3. Martello Tower & Museum of Vintage Radio
4. National Transport Museum
5. Deer Park & Golf Courses
6. Deer Park Hotel
7. Ireland's Eye
8. Howth Head
9. Beshoff Bros

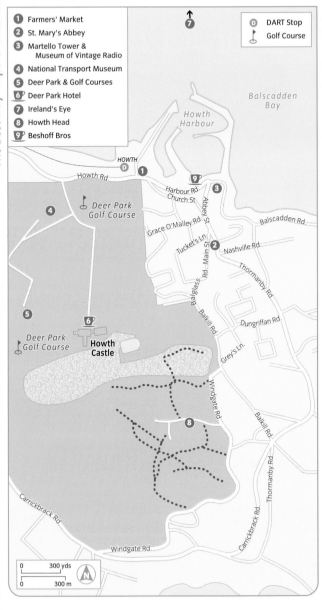

- **D** DART Stop
- Golf Course

Balscadden Bay

Howth Harbour

HOWTH

Howth Rd.

Harbour Rd.
Church St
Grace O'Malley Rd.
Abbey St.
Balscadden Rd.

Tucket's Ln.
St. Mary's Rd.
Nashville Rd.
Thormanby Rd.

Balglass Rd.
Balkill Rd.
Dungriffan Rd.

Deer Park Golf Course

Deer Park Golf Course

Howth Castle

Grey's Ln.

Windgate Rd.

Balkill Rd.
Thormanby Rd.

Carrickbrack Rd.

Carrickbrack Rd.

Windgate Rd.

| 0 | 300 yds |
| 0 | 300 m |

Relaxing Howth is loved for its coastal walks, plus trips to the tiny Ireland's Eye, and a museum housing historic fire engines. Located on the scenic Howth Peninsula, and once an island and sleepy fishing community, Howth is now a busy suburb and huge, prominent fishing center. It's a great trip for children, yet I enjoy Howth as much now as I did as a kid, especially on a Sunday.

START: **DART to Howth.**

❶ ★ Farmers' Market. Located near the West Pier, the busy Sunday market's outdoor stalls are perfect for stocking up on food for the day, or simply jars of homemade pickles and preserves for gifts. Given its huge success (and recent expansion) it's strange to think that markets such as these have only been going since 2005. The indoor section, housed along the West Pier, has rails of clothes and unusual silver jewelry. *Howth Harbour. www. irishfarmersmarkets.ie/howth.html. Sun & bank hol Mon 10am–5pm.*

❷ ★★ St. Mary's Abbey. Take the steep uphill walk from the East Pier to the ruins of St. Mary's Abbey and graveyard, dating back to 1042.

A stunning view of St Mary's Abbey.

Local produce at the Sunday Market.

If nothing else, the view of the waterfront from here is superb. Dedicated to the Virgin Mary, this was a collegiate, indicating that it was served by a college or community of clerics who lived south of the church. It was first built in 1042 by King Sitric of Dublin, replaced in 1235, again in the second half of the 14th century, and later modified. 🕐 *20 mins.*

❸ ★★ Martello Tower & Museum of Vintage Radio. This recently restored Martello Tower is one of 34 dotted along the east coast to ward off pesky Napoleonic invasions. It hosts the quaintly named **Ye Olde Hurdy Gurdy Museum of Vintage Radio**, a personal collection of the delightful Pat Herbert, who is happy to show visitors the old radios, music boxes, gramophones, etc. It's fitting that the two-level museum should be here, because in 1852 one of the world's first cables was laid at this point. It was used by the American Lee de Forrest in 1903 for telegraphy experiments, and in 1905 the Marconi Company conducted ship-to-shore wireless experiments from here. On Sunday mornings, you'll probably see amateur radio station EI0MAR operating at the tower in Morse code. ⏱ *40 min. Martello Tower.* ☎ *086-815 4189. www. ei0mar.org. Admission: €5 adults, €3 seniors, free children 15 and under (must be accompanied by adult). Daily May–Oct 11am–4pm; Nov–Apr by appt.*

④ kids ★★ National Transport Museum. Run by volunteers, this collection has 180 exhibits dating between 1883 and 1984 crammed into a tiny space, rather like squeezing through a crowded car park. With the Hill of Howth tram, the Merryweather steam fire engine, and bakers' vans galore, the huge horde has examples from passenger, emergency, commercial, and military vehicles. Look out for the illuminated tram, Dublin's only one, which toured the city at night advertizing parish fetes, and was badly burnt in the 1930s. Ask museum staff to point out the Merryweather fire-fighter from 1883 (the museum's oldest), the 1889 Merryweather steam pump, and the 1930s Leyland Tiger bus, nicknamed in irony as 'our very own Celtic Tiger'. ⏱ *40 min. Heritage Depot, Howth Demesne.* ☎ *01-832 0427;* ☎ *086-828 9437. www.national transportmuseum.org. Admission: €3 adults, €1.50 children, €8 family. Jun–Aug, Mon–Fri 10am–5pm; Sat, Sun & hols 2–5pm; Sept–May Sat, Sun & hols 2–5pm*

⑤ ★★ Deer Park & Golf Courses. The walk from the Transport Museum takes you through the tranquil Deer Park (although deer remain elusive) past Howth Castle, dating back to 1450. The castle itself

Old-time dream machines at the Transport Museum.

Local resident.

has now been converted into upmarket residences and is not open for public viewing. The **Rhododendron Gardens**, one of Europe's largest, lie a little deeper inside the park, and visitors in May and early June can gaze at the 40 varieties of glorious blooms in reds, pinks, and purples. Inside the park are the golf courses run by the Deer Park Hotel. Visitors can take their pick of very reasonably priced green fees and club hire for the pitch and putt, two 9-hole courses (Grace O'Malley Course and the St. Fintan's Course), and an 18-hole course, the Deer Park. *Deer Park Hotel, Deer Park,* ☎ *01-832 2624;* ☎ *01-832 3489. www.deerpark-hotel.ie. Golf courses daily 7am–7pm; winter 8am–2pm.*

Practical Matters: Howth

Catch the DART 15 kilometers (9 miles) east to Howth, from city center stations including Connolly Station, Tara Street, Pearse, and Grand Canal Dock. Single tickets cost €2.30. Services run approximately every 10 to 15 minutes Monday to Saturday (6:15am–midnight); every 30 minutes Sunday (9am–midnight). Bus nos. 31 and 31B run from the city center, including Connolly Station. The Nitelink 31N night bus travels between Howth and Dublin city center every 30 minutes. **Howth Tourism Information Office**: Ground Floor, 1 West Pier, Howth. ☎ 01-839 6955. www.howthismagic.com. **Hotel:** The scenic Deer Park Hotel offers good rates ☎ 01-832 2624; www.deerpark-hotel.ie. **Restaurants:** Aqua (p 102) is an excellent, stylish fish restaurant.

6 **Deer Park Hotel.** The terrace of the hotel makes for a good stop for tea and scones, while gazing out over the greens. *Deer Park.* ☎ 01-832 2624. $

7 ★★ **Ireland's Eye.** Boats leave regularly during the summer for the tiny island just 2km (1.2 miles) from Howth Harbour. This rocky outcrop is perfect for keen ornithologists and lovers of desolate beaches, dramatic cliffs, and ruined churches. It houses a Martello Tower built in the early 19th century, and the remains of a 6th-century monastic church, part of Howth's long Christian history. It is believed that the *Garland of Howth*, a Latin manuscript of the New Testament, now in Trinity College Library, was written here. Get out the binoculars to spot puffins, kittiwakes, and cormorants, and of course seals. Tread carefully (so you don't stand on eggs) and wander the island. It's hard to believe it's so close to the city. 🕐 *1½ hr. Boats run from East Pier,* ☎ *086-845 9154. www.islandferries.net. Fare €15 adults, €10 children. Please call to*

Fishing boats in Howth harbour.

Howth lighthouse.

check times. Approx 10am–6pm daily; evening in Jun & Jul. No fixed timings, approx every 30 min, takes 15 min.

8 ★★ **Howth Head.** If weather permits and you have enough time (it's no fun if it's too cloudy to see the view), take a walk along the Howth Peninsula coastline, passing the rugged landscape. Its summit is the perfect point to see the peninsula, with the Dublin Mountains in the background. There is a well-marked 4.5 mile (7km) path and large map at East Pier, or take the cliff-side walk. All paths are well trodden, so take whichever one you fancy. I love taking a picnic to the Howth Head for a dining experience with a spectacular view. 🕐 *2 hr.*

9 **Beshoff Bros.** Fish rarely tastes this good. Queue up for fish 'n' chips (try the smoked haddock) with tubs of garlic sauce then savor them, sitting on the pier in the setting sun: inexpensive and wonderful. *Harbour Road.* ☎ 01-832 1754. $. ●

The
Savvy Traveler

Before You Go

Government Tourist Offices
In the U.S.: 345 Park Ave, 17th Floor, New York, NY 10154 (☎ 212-418-0800). Toll-free Infoline ☎ 800-22-6470. **In Canada:** (☎ 800-223-6470. **In the U.K.:** 1 03 Wigmore St, London W1U 1QS (☎ 020-7518 0800). Freephone infoline (☎ 0800-039 7000). **In Australia:** ☎ 02-9299 6177.

The Best Times to Go
June to September is the best and busiest time to visit, with myriad festivals throughout the summer, although as a city break Dublin is popular year round. Hotels are often a little cheaper from **November to February.** There's no particular month to avoid, although be prepared for huge crowds in **March** for the St. Patrick's Day celebrations, a public holiday. The **Christmas** season sees shopping areas packed in the build-up, with special markets opening. It's also a popular destination for **New Year's Eve,** especially to hear the midnight bells peal from Christ Church Cathedral, and see the New Year's Day parade. As Ireland's capital and a base to explore the country, Dublin enjoys year-round tourism plus major sporting events, so mid- to high-range hotels should be booked well in advance.

Festivals & Special Events
SPRING. One of the highlights of the year is **St. Patrick's Day** (17th March), a packed, week-long party throughout the city with a huge parade, music, fairs, and lasers, when every visitor seems to boast Irish roots—however remote. Book your hotel early for this one. ☎ 01-676 3205. www.stpatricks festival.ie.

Temple Bar plays host to the **Dublin Handel Festival,** a week-long series of recitals and workshops celebrating April's anniversary of the world premiere of this musical masterpiece, held in Dublin in 1742. ☎ 01-677 2255. www.templebar.ie.

April or May's **Dublin Dance Festival** has contemporary dance from around the world, with top choreographers, masterclasses, and seminars. ☎ 01-679 0524. www. dublindancefestival.ie. In May the two-week long **International Dublin Gay Theatre Festival** showcases gay contributors to Irish drama, with an emphasis on new works with a gay theme or relevance. ☎ 01 677 8511. www.gaytheatre.ie.

Summer is beckoned in with floral delights in Phoenix Park for **Bloom** (early June), with garden designs, entertainment, and flower shows galore. ☎ 01-668 5155. www.bloominthepark.com. Tall ships, markets, and music show off the ever-changing developing waterfront at the **Docklands Maritime Festival** (early June). www. dublindocklands.ie.

SUMMER. **Temple Bar** hosts a plethora of summer cultural and entertainment events, which usually include outdoor film screenings in the main square, circus, opera, and street theater. ☎ 01-677 2255. www.templebar.ie.

The week-long **Dublin Writers' Festival** (June) gives you a chance to meet international authors and journalists to discuss their work, in various venues; 2009's festival featured luminaries like Seamus Heaney, Colm Tóibín, and Joe Queenan. ☎ 01-222 5455. www. dublinwritersfestival.com.

Useful Websites

www.visitdublin.com: Dublin Tourist Office's official site, with maps, sightseeing, events, accommodation offers, and info on local transport.

www.discoverireland.com: Official site of Tourism Ireland, with information on the entire country, details on airlines flying from the U.S., and golf packages.

www.dublinks.com: Decent guide to events, sightseeing, and nightlife.

www.indublin.ie: Listings of events, comedy, music, theater, and reviews of bars and restaurants.

www.ireland.com: Online version of the excellent *Irish Times* newspaper, including an Ancestors section.

www.independent.ie: The online version of the daily Irish *Independent* newspaper with local and national news and events.

www.whatsonwhen.com: Regularly updated listings of Dublin's events, from the sublime to the ridiculous, including festivals, arts, and events.

www.thedubliner.ie: The online version of the monthly magazine, with food and drink reviews, current affairs, and local arts scene.

www.dublinbus.ie: Timetables, ticket info, and sightseeing tours for Dublin Bus.

www.irishrail.ie: Rail information to get around Ireland, plus DART timetables.

www.tickets.ie: Booking site for tickets for major events, with collection points around the city.

www.118.ie: Directory including shops, offices, and services from acupuncture to zip fasteners.

James Joyce fans get all Edwardian for **Bloomsday** (16th June), re-enacting or listening to his masterpiece *Ulysses* set around Dublin on this day, marking the date when its hero Leopold Bloom goes about his daily business. ☎ 01-878 8547. www.jamesjoyce.ie.

Dublin Pride enjoys two weeks of social and cultural events in June, marking the anniversary of New York's Stonewall Riots, culminating in a huge parade, and getting bigger each year. www.dublinpride.org. The relatively new (since 2004) but well-respected **Oxegen** music festival (July) takes over Punchestown Racecourse in Kildare for a weekend, with a heavyweight line-up of top, mainly British, rock and indie bands. www.oxegen.ie.

The Royal Dublin Society hosts the prestigious **Dublin Horse Show** (August) with five days of top international show-jumping, including the **Aga Khan Challenge Trophy** with international teams. ☎ 01-668 0866. www.dublinhorseshow.com. Port town Dún Laoghaire puts on the wonderful **Festival of World Culture** weekend (July or August) with musicians from nearly

100 countries around the world, quite possibly from Algeria to Zambia, acknowledging Dublin's increasingly multi-ethnic population. ☎ 01-271 9555. www.festivalofworldcultures.com.

The tempo hots up at Croke Park for the **Hurling and Gaelic Football semi-finals** (late Aug) and **final** (early Sept) when the national tournaments reach a climax. Hotels get booked up quickly. ☎ 01-865 8657. www.gaa.ie.

FALL. The fortnight-long **Dublin Fringe Festival** (Sept) has a packed program of international fringe companies in various venues around town, with cabaret, music, theater and more. ☎ 01-817 1677. www.fringefest.com.

The **Dublin Theatre Festival** (Sept–Oct) is Europe's longest-running theater festival, going strong since 1957, and brings top international theater plus new Irish plays, to a variety of venues. ☎ 01-677 8439. www.dublintheatrefestival.com. Ghouls, ghosts, and costumed street artists come out to play for the **Samhain Hallowe'en Parade** (around 31st October) through the city center, originally a pagan festival celebrating the dead and the start of winter, now a public holiday.

WINTER. Christmas does have its spiritual side after all, with traditional Mass and candlelit services at the **Christmas Eve Vigil** at St. Mary's Pro-Cathedral, with music from the famous Palestrina Choir. Then get earthy and blow your Christmas money at the **Christmas Racing Festival** (26th December) at Leopardstown, the start of a four-day festival at one of Ireland's premier racecourses. ☎ 01-289 0500. www.leopardstown.com.

Ring in the **New Year** with Christ Church Bells at midnight, when locals gather to hear Ireland's loudest peals. ☎ 01-677 8099. www.cccdub.ie. Traditional Irish music and culture comes alive at **Temple Bar Trad Fest** (Jan or Feb), where jigs and reels are performed by great musicians in cozy bars and cultural venues. ☎ 01-677 2397. www.templebartrad.com.

The Weather

With a cool, damp climate pretty much year-round, don't come to Dublin for a suntan. The warmest months are June to August, the likeliest time to enjoy sunny spells. In case of a hot spell, most hotels have air-conditioning, if not a fan.

It's important to remember that it can rain at any time; be prepared for it, bring waterproofs, and take on the local cheerful attitude towards the odd shower, treating a sunny day and clear skies as a bonus. After all, this is what makes Ireland as green as it is.

DUBLIN AVERAGE TEMPERATURE & RAINFALL

	JAN	FEB	MAR	APR	MAY	JUN
Daily temp °F	39	41	45	46	50	55
Daily temp °C	4	5	7	8	10	13
Rainfall (inch)	2.7	2.2	2.0	1.8	2.4	2.2
Rainfall (cm)	6.8	5.5	5.1	4.6	6.1	5.7
	JUL	AUG	SEP	OCT	NOV	DEC
Daily temp °F	59	59	55	50	45	43
Daily temp °C	15	15	13	10	7	6
Rainfall (inch)	2.7	2.8	2.8	2.8	2.7	2.8
Rainfall (cm)	6.9	7.2	7.1	7.0	6.8	7.0

The nights draw in early, and winter sets in, from November to February, although the temperature rarely falls to freezing.

Cellphones (mobiles)

Cellphones in the U.S. may be different from those in Ireland (known here as mobiles). For traveling abroad, it may be easier to ensure your phone has GSM technology; most tri-band phones will work over in Ireland and some dual-band (1,800 MHz) may work also. Check with your phone manufacturer. Contact your cellphone server to ensure you have a roaming facility. Bear in mind that phoning, texting, or even receiving calls from your overseas number may be prohibitively expensive. If you travel regularly, it's good U.S. value to buy a new handset (with plenty of low-cost options) from **Carphone Warehouse** 30 Grafton St., (☎ 01-670 5265); or

2 Henry St. (☎ 01-878 470). If your own cellphone is compatible with other sim cards (any unlocked phone will be), you can just buy a local sim card (networks include O2, Vodafone, Meteor, and Three) to make local calls.

Car Rentals

Driving within Dublin is neither advised nor necessary, given the expensive parking, dreadful traffic jams, relatively cheap taxis, and decent bus service. Should you wish to drive farther afield, for example to explore Kildare, Wicklow, or Hill of Tara, it's better to book ahead via Avis, Budget, Hertz, and the like. Most convenient is to book via the Dublin Tourism website (www.visit dublin.com); their section 'Getting Around' includes car hire, with all models and companies displayed on a clear one-page price comparison.

Getting **There**

By Plane

Dublin Airport (☎ 01-814 1111; www.dublinairport.com) underwent a much-needed expansion in 2009 and there will be a high-tech second terminal in operation from late 2010. It is the HQ of budget Irish airline Ryanair, with cheap flights to and from Europe. Long-haul airlines flying to Dublin include Aer Lingus (the national airline), British Airways, American Airlines, Continental, and Air Canada. Short-haul flight operators from the U.K. include BMI and CityJet. There is a greater selection of international routes that involve changing in London, U.K.

From the airport (10km (6.5 miles) north of the city center) there are several ways to get into town, all of which leave from outside the arrivals hall. The double-decker

Airlink (adults €6/children €3) has two services: no. 747 travels via O'Connell Street to Central Bus Station (Busaras) every 10 minutes 5:30am–11pm, taking around 35 minutes. No. 748 also goes via Central Bus Station but ends up at Heuston Railway Station, taking around 45 minutes. The single-decker **Aircoach** (free with pre-purchased **Dublin Pass;** adults €7/children €1) goes to Ballsbridge via O'Connell Street, Grafton Street, and Merrion Square every 10 minutes 6am–8pm, every 20 minutes 8pm–midnight, and every hour through the night. It takes around 45 minutes to reach Grafton St. Slowest and cheapest is the public bus, **Dublin Bus** (€2.20), making frequent stops into town and taking around an hour. **Taxis** wait outside the arrivals hall, with a metered fare into the city center around €25–30, although it's slower and more expensive in rush hour.

It is important to allow plenty of time when traveling to the airport, as traffic is very slow, especially during the after-work rush hour, and on weekends especially when there is a major match at Croke Park.

By Car

The **N11** highway leads to Dublin from Dún Laoghaire harbor (and car ferry), the **N1** and **M1** from Belfast in the north, the **N6 and N4** from Galway in the west, and the **N8** and **N7** from Cork in the south. Signs to **City Centre** (*An Lar*) will clearly be posted as you approach Dublin. From the airport, take the **M1.**

By Train

There are two railway stations in Dublin run by **Irish Rail** (www. irishrail.ie): **Connolly Station** (☎ 01-703 2358) has services to Belfast and Sligo; trains from **Heuston Station** (☎ 01-703 3299) include Cork, Tralee, Limerick, Waterford, Galway, and Kildare. The InterRail Global Pass and InterRail One Country Pass are both valid throughout Ireland. (www.inter railnet.com).

By Ferry

Despite the plethora of cheap flights to Ireland, plenty of car-ferries still operate the Dublin route from the U.K. **Irish Ferries** (☎ 0818-300 400; www.irishferries.com) run speedy car ferries between **Dublin** and **Holyhead** (North Wales) several times a day, plus **Rosslare** and **Pembroke. Norfolkline** (U.K.: ☎ 0844-499 0007; Ireland: ☎ 01-819 2999; www.norfolkline-ferries.co.uk) have day and night sailings between **Liverpool** and **Dublin** taking around seven hours. **Stena Line** (U.K.: ☎ 08705-204 204; Ireland: ☎ 01-204 7777; www. stenaline.co.uk) runs separate services from **Holyhead** to both **Dún Laoghaire** and **Dublin Port. P&O Irish Sea** (U.K.: ☎ 0844 770 7070; Ireland: ☎ 01-204 777; www.poirish sea.com) have two ferries daily between Liverpool and Dublin.

Getting **Around**

By Bus

Sorely missing an underground system, **Dublin Bus** (☎ 01-873 4222; www.dublinbus.ie) network covers most of the city, although it can be overworked and slow-going in rush hour. Pay by exact change only to the driver (always worth having a bundle of coins handy) with fares depending on what stage you board. Most city center journeys cost between €1 and €2, with a special 50c fare within the central zone. If you're doing several journeys, it's worth getting a one-day (€6) or three-day (€13.30) ticket (also valid on the Airlink from Dublin airport; buy it in the arrivals hall), allowing unlimited bus journeys. Timetables and routes are usually displayed at the bus stops. **Nitelink** buses run from 11:30pm Friday and Saturday from the city center to the suburbs, including Howth and Dalkey; flat fare €5.

By Luas

The **Luas** light rail system (☎ 01-461 4910; www.luas.ie) is wonderfully comfortable, good value, and frequent. It's just a shame that the only two lines in the city don't actually meet up. The Green Line runs along the southeast of the city, from

St. Stephen's Green to Sandyford, via Dundrum. The Red Line runs along the north bank of the Liffey from The Point (home of the O2 entertainment venue) via the bus station Busaras with a link to Connolly Station; west through Four Courts and Smithfield to Heuston Station, then down the southwest suburbs to Tallaght. Single and return tickets are bought from the machines on the platform (change given); daily passes are also available.

By DART

The Dublin Area Rapid Transport or **DART** (☎ 01-703 3504; www. irishrail.ie) operates speedy, green trains at great value to coastal areas out of town. The nearest city center stations are Pearse (south of the Liffey) and Connolly (north), taking around 20 minutes to Dún Laoghaire and Howth (€2.30). Buy tickets from the machines or ticket counter at the station; a one-day pass works out cheaper if making more than two longer journeys.

By Taxi

Taxis are plentiful and relatively cheap in Dublin; just flag one down on the street. There are private hire cab offices all around the city; every hotel, restaurant, bar, and club will probably have the number of their local one. Evening taxi ranks include Dame Street opposite College Green, and another near City Hall, Dawson Street opposite Mansion House, Merrion Row near St. Stephen's Green, and St. Andrew Street outside the post office. All taxis are on the meter, starting at around €3.80 (€4.10 8pm–8am and Sundays) with an extra €2.50 if booked in advance.

On Foot

Dublin is the perfect walking city, with most places of interest in the small, compact center. It is also a city where the getting from A to B is half the fun, discovering unexpected delights along the way. Bring comfortable walking shoes, be prepared for showers, and try and do as much as possible on foot.

Fast **Facts**

APARTMENT RENTALS **Gulliver Ireland** (☎ 066-979 2030; www. gulliver.ie) is a good agency for renting apartments and holiday homes in the Dublin area; the **Dublin Tourism** website has deals for self-catering accommodations (www. visitdublin.com). The official **Tourism Ireland** website (www.discover ireland.com) lists serviced apartments and town houses, including in the city center.

ATMS/CASHPOINTS Most banks have 24-hour ATMs, which accept Maestro, Cirrus, and Visa cards, and are found especially in the main shopping areas. Exchange currency either at banks or travel agents like Thomas Cook; check the rates of all exchange offices as rates and commission vary. There is usually a small transaction fee for any overseas card, plus a probable additional fee from your bank back home. Major Irish banks include Bank of Ireland, Allied Irish Bank, and Ulster Bank. (See also Money.)

BUSINESS HOURS Banks are open Monday–Friday, 10am–4pm, with most open till 5pm on Thursday. Most offices are open Monday–Friday 10am–5pm. At restaurants, lunch is usually noon–3pm and dinner 7pm–10:30pm. Major stores are

The Savvy Traveler

open Monday–Saturday 9:30/10am–6pm; late-night shopping on Thursday till 8pm; Sundays from 11am–4/5pm, although not all stores are open on Sundays. Most museums close one day a week, usually on Mondays, including the National Museums.

CONSULATES & EMBASSIES **U.S. Embassy,** 42 Elgin Rd, Ballsbridge (☎ 01-668 8777; http://dublin. usembassy.gov); **Canadian Embassy,** 7–8 Wilton Terrace, (☎ 01-234 4000; www.canada.ie); **British Embassy,** 29 Merrion Rd, Ballsbridge (☎ 01-205 3700; http:// britishembassyinireland.fco.gov.uk); **Australian Embassy,** 7th Floor, Fitzwilton House, Wilton Terrace (☎ 01-664 5300; www.ireland. embassy.gov.au).

CREDIT CARDS   Call your credit card company the minute you discover it has been lost or stolen to cancel the card, and file a report at the nearest police station (Garda). To report loss or theft of **American Express** cards from Ireland, U.S. residents should call Global Assist on ☎ 001-715-343-7977; U.K. residents call ☎ 1850-882-028. To report a stolen **Visa** card for the U.K., ☎ +44 (0)1273-696 933; US ☎ 1-800-55-8002. Your PIN is required when using your credit card at all outlets, rather than signing.

DOCTORS   Ask your hotel for a local doctor.

ELECTRICITY   Most hotels operate on 230 volts AC (50 cycles), three-pin plugs. Adaptors can be provided at major hotels.

EMERGENCIES   Dial ☎ 999 for police, ambulance, or fire emergencies. (See also Insurance, below.)

GAY & LESBIAN TRAVELERS   Dublin's city center isn't on a par with New York's Greenwich Village or London's Soho for gay lifestyle, but it's relatively liberal compared with the suburbs. There are very few specifically gay bars and clubs, although other venues have gay nights which attract a mixed friendly crowd. The social scene has grown and improved over recent years, although outward displays of same-sex affection aren't particularly the done thing. **Gay Community News** (www.gcn.ie) is a guide to what's on in the city, in particular 'In & Out'. October's **International Dublin Gay Theatre Festival** (☎ 01-677 8511; www.gaytheatre.ie) was established to commemorate the 150th anniversary of the birth of Oscar Wilde, Dublin's most celebrated gay man.

GOLF   There are a great number of stunning golf courses scattered around the region. Dublin Tourism offers two **golf packages**, including three rounds of golf at different courses at much reduced rates. Choose between mountain views, links courses, and stunning parkland. www.visitdublin.com.

HOLIDAYS   Public holidays: 1st January (New Year's Day), 17th March (St. Patrick's Day), March/April (Good Friday and Easter Monday), first Mon in May (May Day), first Mon in June (June Bank Holiday), first Mon in August (August Bank Holiday), last Mon in October (Hallowe'en), 25th December (Christmas Day), 26th December (St. Stephen's Day).

INSURANCE   Check your existing insurance policies before buying travel insurance to cover trip cancellation, lost luggage, medical expenses, or car rental insurance. In the U.S., recommended insurers include: **Access America** (☎ 1-800-284-8300; www.accessamerica. com); **Travel Assistance International** (☎ 1-800-821-2828;

www.travelassistance.com); and for medical insurance **MEDEX Assistance** (☎ 1-800-732-5309; www.medexassist.com). U.K. and E.U. residents should take a **European Health Insurance Card** (EHIC; formerly the E-111), for free or heavily discounted emergency medical treatment within the E.U. ID should also be brought if requiring emergency medical treatment.

INTERNET   Internet access is widespread: in cybercafes, convenience stores, and small spaces above shops which also offer cheap international calls. Many have Skype facilities. Most hotels offer Wi-Fi or broadband in their rooms, and there is an increasing amount of Wi-Fi hotspots in the city center.

LANGUAGE   Ireland has two official languages—English and Gaelic—although in Dublin everyone speaks English. All signs in state-run public places (stations, street names etc) are legally required to be in Gaelic also. Look out for signs on the toilets—*Mna* actually means 'women'!

LEFT LUGGAGE LOCKERS   There are 24-hour luggage lockers in the basement of Busáras; Heuston Station has lockers 7am to 10pm; Connolly station does not, although opposite the reliable HHT Internet & Call Shop (16 Amiens St.; open 9am–midnight) offers the service for €5 per large item.

LOST PROPERTY   If your luggage gets lost in transit from a flight, contact your airline at the airport. For all thefts, report to a local police station (Garda). For loss or theft of credit cards, see *Credit Cards* above. Other useful numbers: **Bus Eireann** (Central Bus Station) ☎ 01-836 6111; **Dublin Bus** ☎ 01-703 1321. **Heuston Station** ☎ 01-703 2332; **Connolly Station** ☎ 01-703 2358; **Taxi** ☎ 01-666 9851.

MAIL & POSTAGE   Mail boxes are green, post offices are called An Post. Most famous of all is the **General Post Office,** O'Connell St. ☎ 01-705 8833, opening hours Mon–Sat 8:30am–6pm. For **Poste Restante** collection, bring photo ID. Other city center post offices include: 16 Merrion Row, ☎ 01-676 5961 and 1A Earlsfort Terrace, ☎ 01-662 3192. Opening hours for both are Monday–Friday 9am–1pm and 2:15–5:30pm; Saturday 9am–1pm. A letter or postcard sent within Ireland costs €.55; to the U.S., U.K., or rest of the world €.82.

MONEY   The single European currency in Ireland is the **Euro,** which is used in 14 other European countries (not the U.K.). At press time, the exchange rate was approximately €1 = $1.37 (or £.88). For up-to-the-minute exchange rates, check the currency converter website **www.xe.com.** Euros are available at all ATMs and exchange booths. The main Tourist Office on Suffolk St. has a Fexco Bureau de Change.

PASSPORTS   No visas are required for U.S., U.K., Canadian, Australian, or New Zealand visitors to Ireland, for stays of up to 90 days. If your passport is lost or stolen, contact your country's embassy or consulate immediately (see Consulates & Embassies, above). Make a copy of your passport's critical pages before you leave and keep it in a safe place.

PHARMACIES   Pharmacies operate during normal business hours, with a green cross clearly displayed outside, and some open till 10pm in the city center. There are no all-night pharmacies. **City Pharmacy** (14 Dame St., ☎ **01-670 4523**) is open Mon–Sat until 10pm. **Boots the Chemist** (20 Henry St., ☎ **01-873 0209**; Unit 113, St. Stephen's Green, ☎ **01-478 4368**; 12 Grafton St.,

☎ **01-677 3000**) is open until 7pm to 9pm most nights except Sunday.

POLICE The national police (Garda) emergency number is ☎ **999** or ☎ **112**. Local police stations in the city include **Pearse Street** (☎ **01-666 9000**); **Store Street** (☎ **01-666 8000**); and **Harcourt Terrace** (☎ **01-666 9500**).

SAFETY Take the usual precautions in major cities: watch your bags and valuables in busy places and keep cash and wallets out of sight; avoid walking in dark, quiet areas alone at night, including Phoenix Park; shield your PIN and take the cash away quickly from the ATM; keep money out of your back pocket. Most crime is drink- or drug-related, with drunken revelers a common sight in the city center at weekends. If in doubt, avoid crowds like these. Drug dealers have been known to hang around the Liffey Boardwalk; look confident and don't make eye contact.

SMOKING Smoking has been banned on all public transport and in other public places since 2004. Locals seem to have adapted well to the ban in pubs, clubs, and restaurants, with a noticeable improvement to outside spaces and terraces.

TAXES Value-added tax (VAT) is 21% on most goods, excluding food, books, and children's clothes. Most hotels include tax when quoting the price. Non-E.U. residents are entitled to a reimbursement of VAT, at shops with the **Global Refund Tax Free Shopping** sign displayed. Ask the shop assistant for the Global Refund Cheque (there is no minimum spend for this), get it stamped, and take it to your last port of call when leaving the E.U. (in this case usually Dublin Airport). Get your cash (or credit card) refund at the

Global Refund office at the airport before you fly. For more information see www.globalrefund.com.

TELEPHONES For national directory enquiries, ☎ **11811**; for international ☎ **11818**. Telephone boxes dot the city, either coin-operated or with pre-paid phonecards (available from newsagents and post offices). The code for Dublin is ☎ **01**, not required if you are calling from Dublin except from a mobile phone. To make an international call, dial ☎ **00**, then the country code. Calls from hotels are far more expensive than calling from outside; look for the (ever increasing) call offices offering cheap rates to call overseas.

TIPPING Service charge is not usually added to the check (but do make sure), and so it's customary to leave a tip of between 10–12%, more if the service has been great. If paying by credit card, it is recommended to leave a cash tip, which is more likely to go to the service staff rather than management. For small cafes and snacks, a few coins or rounded up to the nearest euro is usual. With taxi drivers, a small tip is welcome but not necessary, and a small tip is always welcome (but not obligatory) for hotel porters and cleaners.

TOILETS It's easy to avoid unappealing public toilets by running into hotels, bars, shopping centers, fast-food restaurants, and department stores instead.

TOURIST INFORMATION **Dublin Tourism** ☎ **01-605 7700**. Offices: Suffolk St. (main office), Monday–Saturday 9am–5:30pm, Sunday 10:30am–3pm; July & August, Monday–Saturday 9am–7pm, Sunday 10:30am–3pm. Also on Upper O'Connell St.: 9am–5pm. Both offices have bookings, maps, reservations, a gift shop, all-Ireland information, and an accommodation reservations service. There is an information desk at the arrivals hall in Dublin Airport.

TRAVELERS WITH DISABILITIES Restaurants, hotels, buses, and stations are increasingly accessible to wheelchair users, which must adhere to E.U. regulations. All new buildings take wheelchair access into account; you may find that older buildings do less so. Most taxi companies will have some vehicles that can access wheelchairs; phone to check. Phone ahead when visiting restaurants and hotels to confirm their facilities. Useful organizations include the **Irish Wheelchair Association** (www.iwa.ie) and **National Disability Authority** (www.nda.ie).

Dublin: **A Brief History**

600 B.C .The Celts first arrive in Ireland.

A.D. 432 St. Patrick arrives in Ireland and establishes the first Roman Catholic church—perhaps at the site of St. Patrick's Cathedral—and converts the Irish.

837 The Vikings arrive in Dublin, using the permanent settlement as a base to plunder surrounding regions.

1014 Brian Boru, high King of Ireland, defeats the Vikings at the battle of Clontarf.

1169 The Normans capture Dublin, led by Strongbow.

1541 Henry VIII is declared King of Ireland, and tries to introduce Protestantism.

1649 Oliver Cromwell's army lands in Dublin, and then kills thousands in Drogheda. Land is taken from Catholic landowners and distributed around Cromwell's Protestant supporters.

1695 Penal laws restrict education for Catholics and prohibit them from buying property.

1727 Catholics deprived of the right to vote.

1759 Guinness Brewery is established in St. James's Gate.

1801 The Act of Union joins England to Ireland, prohibiting Catholics from holding public office.

1829 Daniel O'Connell, a Catholic lawyer, organizes the Catholic Association, helping to achieve the Catholic Emancipation Act.

1845–8 The Great Potato Famine: over a million people die and more emigrate on America-bound boats from Dublin's docks.

1904 The Abbey Theatre opens.

1913 Jim Larkin, head of the Trade Union movement, leads the workers in the Great Lockout.

1914 Outbreak of World War I, delaying implementation of new Home Rule legislation.

1916 Nationalists stage Easter Rising, seizing the GPO and proclaiming an independent Irish Republic. The British crush the rising and most of its leaders are executed.

1919–21 The Irish War of Independence against Britain; Eamon de Valera leads the nationalist movement Sinn Féin.

1920 British Parliament passes Government of Ireland Act, with one parliament for the six counties of Northern Ireland and one for the rest of Ireland.

1921 Anglo-Irish Treaty establishes the Irish Free State, partitioned from Northern Ireland.

1922 Dublin Parliament ratifies the treaty, leading to civil war between the IRA and Free State army, killing hundreds. Michael Collins assassinated.

1923 Irish Free State joins the League of Nations.

1926 De Valera founds Fianna Fáil.

1927 De Valera enters Parliament leading Fianna Fáil.

1932 Fianna Fáil wins General Election with de Valera head of government, and tries to eliminate British influence in Irish Free State.

1937 Fianna Fáil wins another election, and Irish Free State is abolished, proclaiming Eire (Gaelic for Ireland) as a sovereign state, with 32 counties.

1938 Douglas Hyde becomes first President of Eire; de Valera is first Prime Minister.

1939 Outbreak of World War II; Eire remains neutral but many Irish citizens join the Allied Forces.

1948 Fianna Fáil loses General Election; Dublin Parliament passes Republic of Ireland Bill.

1949 Easter Monday, anniversary of 1916 Uprising, Eire becomes Republic of Ireland and leaves the British Commonwealth.

1955 Ireland joins the United Nations, but not NATO because of Northern Ireland's status as part of the U.K.

1959 De Valera becomes President of the Republic of Ireland.

1963 U.S. President John F. Kennedy visits Dublin.

1973 Ireland joins the European Economic Community (later known as the European Union).

1980s Dublin suffers the effects of severe economic problems, with high unemployment and rising debts. Many emigrate for better opportunities.

1985 Anglo-Irish Agreement is signed, giving Republic of Ireland a role in the government of Northern Ireland.

1986 Irish budget airline Ryanair's first flight from Dublin to London, quickly spreading routes to and from Europe and increasing tourism.

1990 Mary Robinson becomes first woman President of Ireland.

1991 Ireland signs the Treaty on European Union at Maastricht.

1990s Dublin booms: economic prosperity transforms Ireland (characterized as the Celtic Tiger) from one of Europe's poorest nations to one of its most successful. A time of immigration, rather than emigration.

1992 Ireland votes to loosen the strict abortion law, allowing travel abroad for an abortion.

1993 Downing Street Declaration: Irish and British prime ministers begin the peace process on Northern Ireland.

1997 Divorce becomes legal in Ireland, although opposed by the Roman Catholic Church. The IRA declares a new cease-fire.

1998 Dublin Corporation marks the year as Dublin Millennium, having seized upon the date of A.D. 998 to be when Norse King Glun Iariann agreed to pay taxes.

1998 Good Friday Agreement (also known as the Belfast Agreement) signed between the British and Irish governments, seen as a major development in the Northern Ireland peace process.

2002 The Euro replaces the punt as Ireland's currency.

2004 Smoking is banned in all public places, including bars and restaurants. Publicans fear that this will lead to a drop in revenue.

2004 Ireland, holder of the E.U. presidency, welcomes 10 new member states. Dublin sees the start of a growth of Polish workers.

2007 Bertie Ahern wins third term in office as Prime Minister, and forms a coalition. Green Party enters government for the first time.

2009 Ireland falls into 'the worst recession in the developed world', according to the IMF, with more than 10% unemployment in Dublin. The national soccer team is eliminated from the 2010 World Cup qualifiers by France thanks to a Thierry Henry handball.

2010 The Aviva Stadium opens, the rebuilt Lansdowne Road ground which hosts international rugby and soccer.

Dublin's **Architecture**

Medieval (12th–13th centuries A.D.)

Although the Vikings most certainly made their presence felt after their arrival in the 9th century, little remains of anything so early. In fact, most remains of the Viking settlement were only discovered during the 'Battle of Wood Quay', when Dublin Corporation unearthed the site in the 1970s during excavation, but then insisted on building over it despite huge public pressure.

The grand **Christ Church Cathedral** existed from the Viking times, but was rebuilt by the Normans in the 12th century. The earliest sections surviving are the transept and the crypt, which extends the full length of the cathedral, and once contained three chapels. The Romanesque doorway on the south transept has intricate Irish stonework. Nearby **St. Patrick's Cathedral** was built in the 13th century but, again, has been constructed so many times that little remains of its medieval past, apart from the Romanesque door. Only

the section of the choir gives a hint of the old style. **St. Audoen's Church** is Dublin's oldest surviving church, containing part of the original city wall. St. Audoen's Arch, in its grounds, is the last surviving entrance to the old city.

Post Restoration (17th–18th centuries)

Ireland's first great classical building was **Royal Hospital Kilmainham,** inspired by Hôtel des Invalides in Paris, designed by **William Robinson,** and now home to the Irish Museum of Modern Art. A huge quadrangle built around a courtyard, it has an arcade at ground level. Similar in style is the flat-fronted **Collins Barracks,** built in the early 18th century by **Thomas Burgh,** his first recorded building, with arcaded colonnades on two sides of the square. After the Royal Hospital, this was Dublin's earliest public building. Robinson then created the facade of the small but perfectly formed **Marsh's Library,** typical of a 17th-century scholar's library with decorative oak bookcases.

Georgian (18th century)

Dublin is best known for Georgian architecture, and its enduring image is of flat-fronted, brick, four- or five-floor terraces, usually planned around a private (as then) square. A time when the affluent Protestant gentry were only too happy to improve the city, it was the symmetry and harmony of classical architecture that formed the basis for this style. The **Gardiner** family was the most influential of the private developers, and laid out Parnell Square, Mountjoy Square, and Henrietta Street, which meant the north side was, for a short time, the city's most fashionable area. The city's town houses were brick-built with a basement and symmetrically arranged windows that got shorter higher up to give the illusion of greater height. The best examples today can be seen at **Merrion Square,** which these days is very much a *des res* area. The fanlights over the front doors, and how ornate they were, indicated the wealth and prestige of the owner. They may have looked unadorned from the outside, but plasterers *extraordinaires* enhanced everything, such as **La Franchini** brothers (Newman House).

In addition to the residential squares and terraces, the era was also marked by **James Gandon's Custom House** and the **Four Courts**, both on the Liffey's north bank. Both of these grand buildings were built in the classical style with domes, ornate decoration, and symbolic sculpture adorning the gateways.

Notable architects of the time were German-born **Richard Cassels,** who worked on the **Houses of Parliament,** and **Leinster House,** built for the Earl of Kildare. **Sir Edward**

Lovett Pearce is the main man behind Palladianism in Ireland, including the **Houses of Parliament** (now the Bank of Ireland).

Victorian (19th century)

There are relatively few Victorian masterpieces around the city, as Dublin suffered a decline following the Act of Union, but those that remain make their mark. The stunning red-brick **George's Street Arcade** was Dublin's first and only Victorian shopping center, with ornate Gothic exterior. Traditional bars are the best way of seeing Victorian architecture and interior design; those with rarely changed Victorian interiors include **Ryan's** and the **Stag's Head,** all mahogany paneling and snugs to keep the drinking discrete.

Modern (20th century to present)

The most (in)famous new addition to Dublin's architectural scene is **The Spire,** causing mayhem when it was completed in 2002 to mark the new Millennium (late). The stainless steel spire is 120m (366 ft) high and the tallest structure in Dublin. Other slightly less controversial contemporary creations include the **IFSC,** the International Financial Services Centre, the modern-day powerhouse of Ireland's vibrant economy (although losing its power since the 2008 recession), and the first phase of the Dublin Corporation Offices by Sam Stephenson, one of Dublin's best known contemporary architects. New creations around the docklands, among its sea of glass apartments, mainly empty, include **Grand Canal Square,** designed by **Martha Schwartz.** Within the square, **Grand Canal Theatre,** designed by another U.S. supremo Daniel Libeskind, opened in March 2010, and is loved for its angular-themed exterior in glass and steel.

Dublin's **Movies & Literature**

To get the most out of Dublin's literary heritage, a trip to the theater will give you the best introduction to playwrights like **Oscar Wilde** and his acerbic depictions of middle-class life, **Samuel Beckett** with his abstract interpretation on the complexities of life, and **George Bernard Shaw**, who wrote classics like *Pygmalion*.

If you want to pick up a holiday read, a good starting point to one of the world's most written-about cities is the stream-of-consciousness in **James Joyce**'s *Ulysses*, although the 14 short stories in *Dubliners* might be a little more approachable.

For a touch more hard-edged reality, **Brendan Behan**'s famous *Borstal Boy* (originally written in Irish) is his semi-autobiographical account of his upbringing and membership of the IRA—plus his stint in jail. Likewise the witty yet acerbic *The Quare Fellow* is set in Mountjoy Prison featuring three generations of inmates.

Although abridged as a children's classic, **Jonathan Swift**'s *Gulliver's Travels* (written in Marsh's Library, p 11, ⑫ in the 1720s) is actually a social satire and parody of popular travelogues of the day.

For more contemporary writers, **Roddy Doyle** wrote a series of Dublin-based novels, including light-hearted, music-themed *The Commitments*, and *Paddy Clarke Ha Ha Ha* about a young lad's life on a North-side estate.

Other much-loved local authors include **Maeve Binchy** (try the short story collection *Dublin 4*) and **Edna O'Brien**, who preferred whimsical stories of country life.

Recent movies on Irish history include the much-acclaimed biopic of the Irish rebel *Michael Collins* (dir. Neil Jordan) and *The Wind That Shakes the Barley* (dir. Ken Loach) about the IRA's war against the British, and later the civil war, in the 1920s.

Transport **Numbers & Websites**

Airlines

AER ARANN
☎ 0818-210 210 (Ireland)
☎ 0870-876 7676 (U.K.)
www.aerarann.com

AER LINGUS
☎ 800-474 7424 (U.S. & Canada)
☎ 0818-365 000 (Ireland)
☎ 0871-718 5000 (U.K.)
www.aerlingus.com

*AIR SOUTHWEST
☎ 0870-241 8202 (U.K.)
www.airsouthwest.com

AMERICAN AIRLINES
☎ 800-433 7300 (U.S.)
☎ 01-602 0550 (Ireland)
www.aa.com

*BMI
☎ 800-788 0555 (U.S.)
☎ 01-283 0700 (Ireland)
☎ 0870-607 0555 (U.K.)
www.flybmi.com

BRITISH AIRWAYS
☎ 800-247 9297 (U.S.)
☎ 1890-626 747 (Ireland)
☎ 0844-493 0787 (U.K.)
www.ba.com

*CITYJET
☎ 01-870 0170 (Ireland)
☎ 0871-666 5050 (U.K.)
www.cityjet.com

CONTINENTAL AIRLINES
☎ 800-231 0856 (U.S.)
☎ 1890-925 252 (Ireland)
www.continental.com

DELTA AIRLINES
☎ 800-241 4141 (U.S.)
☎ 01-407 3165 (Ireland)
www.delta.com

*FLYBE
☎ 0871-522 6100 (U.K.)
www.flybe.com

QANTAS
☎ 800-227 4500 (U.S.)
☎ 01-407 3278 (Ireland)
www.qantas.com

*RYANAIR
☎ 0818-303030 (Ireland)
☎ 0871-246 0000 (U.K.)
www.ryanair.com

UNITED AIRLINES
☎ 800-538 2929 (U.S.)
www.united.com

U.S. AIRWAYS
☎ 800-622 1015 (U.S.)
☎ 1890-925 065 (Ireland)
www.usairways.com.
* indicates an Internet-based airline.

Car-hire agencies in Ireland
ALAMO
☎ 877-222 9075 (U.S.)
☎ 01-812 2800 (Dublin Airport)
www.alamo.com

AVIS
☎ 800-230 4898 (U.S.)
☎ 021-428 1111 (Ireland)
☎ 08700-100 287 (U.K.)
www.avis.com
BUDGET
☎ 800-472 3325 (U.S.)
☎ 01-844 5150 (Dublin Airport) www.budget.com
NATIONAL
☎ 800-227 3876 (U.S.)
☎ 01-844 4162 (Ireland)
www.nationalcar.co.uk

SIXT
☎ 01-812 0410 (Dublin Airport)
www.sixt.co.uk
THRIFTY
☎ 800-367 2277 (U.S.)
☎ 01-844 1950 (Dublin Airport)
www.thrifty.com

Index

See also Accommodations and Restaurant indexes, below.

Photo **Credits**